MASTERING ANSIBLE

A Comprehensive Guide to Automating
Configuration Management and Deployment

Ghada Atef

To my family, who have always supported and encouraged me to pursue my dreams. Without their love and unwavering support, this book would not have been possible.

"Automation is not about removing human involvement altogether, it's about freeing up time and energy for creativity and innovation. Ansible is a powerful tool that can help us achieve this goal."

ANONYMOUS

CONTENTS

PREFACE

As the complexity of IT infrastructure grows, the need for efficient and reliable automation tools becomes more pressing. Ansible, a simple yet powerful configuration management and deployment tool has gained widespread popularity for its ease of use, flexibility, and robustness.

This book, "**Mastering Ansible:** *A Comprehensive Guide to Automating Configuration Management and Deployment*", aims to provide a comprehensive and practical guide to mastering Ansible and leveraging its full potential in real-world scenarios. Whether you're a system administrator, a developer, or a DevOps engineer, this book will help you automate repetitive tasks, ensure consistent configurations across your infrastructure, and deploy applications quickly and reliably.

In this book, you'll learn how to:

- Install and configure Ansible and its dependencies
- Write and organize playbooks to define your infrastructure as code
- Use Ansible modules, plugins, and roles to automate complex tasks
- Manage variables, templates, and conditionals in your playbooks
- Leverage dynamic inventory to manage large and heterogeneous environments

- Secure and troubleshoot your Ansible setup
- Examples of how Ansible can be integrated with other tools and systems, and more

Each chapter is structured to provide a step-by-step guide to a specific Ansible topic, with clear explanations, code examples, and best practices. Throughout the book, we'll use real-world scenarios to illustrate how Ansible can help you solve common problems and streamline your workflow.

Whether you're a beginner or an experienced user, this book will help you become a master of Ansible and take your automation skills to the next level. Let's dive in!

PROLOGUE

Imagine you're a system administrator tasked with managing a large and heterogeneous infrastructure. You have dozens of servers, running different operating systems and applications, spread across multiple data centers and cloud providers. You need to ensure that all servers are properly configured, secure, and up-to-date, and that new applications can be deployed quickly and reliably. You also need to keep up with the latest security patches, software releases, and compliance requirements. How do you manage all of this without spending endless hours on repetitive tasks?

This is where Ansible comes in. Ansible is a powerful and flexible configuration management and deployment tool that allows you to automate your infrastructure as code. With Ansible, you can define your infrastructure as a set of playbooks and roles, which describe the desired state of your servers and applications. You can then use Ansible to enforce this desired state, ensuring that all servers are consistent, secure, and up-to-date.

But Ansible is much more than a simple automation tool. It's a philosophy, a way of thinking about infrastructure management that emphasizes simplicity, transparency, and collaboration. Ansible allows you to abstract away the complexity of your infrastructure and focus on the outcomes you want to achieve. It encourages you to write code that is reusable, modular, and testable, and to share your code with others in the community. It enables you to work more efficiently and effectively, and to have more time and energy for creative and innovative work.

In this book, "**Mastering Ansible**: *A Comprehensive Guide to Automating Configuration Management and Deployment*", we'll explore Ansible in depth and show you how to leverage its full potential in real-world scenarios. We'll cover the basics of Ansible, such as installation, configuration, and writing playbooks. We'll also dive into more advanced topics, such as modules, plugins, roles, and dynamic inventory. We'll use real-world scenarios to illustrate how Ansible can help you automate tasks such as deploying applications, managing users and permissions, and provisioning infrastructure. And we'll provide best practices, tips, and tricks to help you become a master of Ansible.

Whether you're a system administrator, a developer, or a DevOps engineer, this book will help you unlock the full power of Ansible and take your infrastructure automation skills to the next level. Let's get started!

CONTACT ME

I'd love to hear from you! Whether you have questions, feedback, please don't hesitate to reach out. Here are a few ways to get in touch:

Email: Feel free to drop me an email at [linux.expert.eg@gmail.com].
I'll do my best to respond as promptly as possible.

Social Media: You can also connect with me on social media platforms. Find me on LinkedIn [Ghada Atef]:
(https://www.linkedin.com/in/ghada-atef/).

Feedback: If you've spotted any errors in the book, have suggestions for improvement, or want to share your success story, please reach out. Your feedback is invaluable!

I'm here to support you on your journey to learn Ansible. Don't hesitate to reach out with your questions, or insights.

Happy learning, and best of luck on your learning journey!

Best Regards,
Ghada Atef

I. INTRODUCTION

In today's fast-paced and ever-changing IT landscape, automation is becoming more important than ever. With increasing demands for faster deployments, greater scalability, and better consistency, organizations are turning to tools like Ansible to help them streamline their operations.

Ansible is a powerful automation tool that allows you to manage and configure servers, network devices, and cloud infrastructure with ease. Whether you're a system administrator, network engineer, or software developer, Ansible can help you automate repetitive tasks, reduce human error, and increase efficiency.

This book is designed to provide you with a comprehensive guide to using Ansible for configuration management and deployment. I'll start with the basics of Ansible, including installation and configuration, and then move on to more advanced topics like playbook creation, inventory management, and cloud automation.

Throughout the book, I'll provide real-world examples and practical advice to help you master Ansible and become more effective in your role. By the end of the book, you'll have a solid understanding of Ansible and its capabilities, as well as the skills you need to automate your infrastructure and applications.

So, whether you're just getting started with Ansible or looking to take your automation skills to the next level, this book has everything you need to become an Ansible expert.

1.1 Explanation of Ansible and its benefits

An overview of Ansible and its benefits!

Ansible is an open-source automation tool that simplifies the management of complex IT infrastructure. It uses a declarative language to define infrastructure configuration and automation tasks, enabling IT teams to streamline their workflow and reduce the time and effort required to manage large-scale systems. In this section, I will discuss what Ansible is, how it works, and its benefits.

What is Ansible?

Ansible is an open-source automation tool that you can use to manage, configure, and deploy software applications across multiple servers. It can help you manage your IT infrastructure, from servers to network devices and everything in between. It uses a simple and powerful language called YAML, which makes it easy to write playbooks that define the tasks you want to automate. With Ansible, you can automate repetitive tasks, manage configuration files, deploy applications, configure servers, manage networks, and more.

Ansible is built on a client-server architecture, where the client (control node) is used to manage the servers or devices that are being controlled. The control node uses SSH (Secure Shell) to connect to the managed nodes (hosts) and perform the required tasks.

How does Ansible work?

Ansible works by executing tasks on managed nodes using Ansible modules. These modules are pre-built scripts that can be used to perform specific tasks, such as installing packages, configuring files, managing users, and more.

The Ansible control node communicates with managed nodes using SSH, which allows it to execute commands and scripts on remote machines. Ansible uses a YAML-based syntax to define the desired state of the infrastructure and then executes the necessary tasks to achieve that state.

Benefits of Ansible

1. **Automation:** Ansible helps automate repetitive tasks, reducing the need for manual intervention and saving time and effort.

2. **Scalability:** You can use Ansible to manage large-scale systems, making it ideal for organizations with complex IT infrastructure.

3. **Consistency:** Ansible ensures that all systems are configured and managed consistently, reducing the risk of configuration errors and improving system reliability.

4. **Flexibility:** You can use Ansible to manage a wide range of systems, including servers, network devices, and cloud resources.

5. **Easy to learn:** Ansible uses a simple syntax and is easy to learn, making it accessible to users with varying levels of experience.

6. **Community support:** Ansible has a large and active community, with many resources available to help users get started and troubleshoot issues.

Conclusion

Ansible is a powerful automation tool that can simplify the management of complex IT infrastructure. Its declarative language and client-server architecture make it easy to use and highly scalable. With its ability to automate repetitive tasks, improve consistency, and increase system reliability, Ansible is a valuable tool for any organization looking to streamline its IT operations.

I.II Ansible and Python

What is the relation between Ansible and Python?
Ansible is a configuration management tool that is written in Python and uses a domain-specific language called YAML to define its playbooks.

Ansible uses Python as its default language for writing modules, which are small pieces of code that interact with different systems and resources.

Python is also used by Ansible to run the playbooks and execute the modules. Ansible's use of Python allows for flexibility, extensibility, and ease of use, as Python has a vast ecosystem of libraries and tools that can be used to interact with different systems and APIs.

Overall, Python plays a critical role in the functioning of Ansible, as it provides the language and ecosystem that Ansible uses to automate infrastructure management.

How to set up Python on RHEL 9?
To set up Python on Red Hat Enterprise Linux (RHEL) 9, you can follow these steps:

Step 1: Check if Python is already installed by running the following command in the terminal:
```
$ python3 --version
```
If Python is not installed, you can skip to step 2. If Python is already installed, you can skip to step 4.

Step 2: Install Python by running the following command in the terminal:
```
$ sudo dnf install python3
```
This will install the latest version of Python 3 that is available in the RHEL 9 repository.

Step 3: Check the version of Python that was installed by running the following command in the terminal:
$ python3 --version
This should display the version number of Python 3 that was installed.

Step 4: Install pip by running the following command in the terminal:
$ sudo dnf install python3-pip
This will install pip, which is a package manager for Python.

Step 5: Check the version of pip that was installed by running the following command in the terminal:
$ pip3 --version
This should display the version number of the pip that was installed.

After completing these steps, Python and pip should be set up on your RHEL 9 system. You can install any additional Python libraries that you need using pip.

How to set up Python on Ubuntu 22.04?
To set up Python on Ubuntu 22.04, you can follow these steps:

Step 1: Open a terminal window by pressing *Ctrl+Alt+T*.

Step 2: Update the package list by running the following command:
$ sudo apt update

Step 3: Install Python 3 by running the following command:
$ sudo apt install python3
This will install the latest version of Python 3 that is available in the Ubuntu 22.04 repository.

Step 4: Check the version of Python that was installed by running

the following command:
$ python3 --version
This should display the version number of Python 3 that was installed.

Step 5: Install pip by running the following command:
$ sudo apt install python3-pip
This will install pip, which is a package manager for Python.

Step 6: Check the version of pip that was installed by running the following command:
$ pip3 --version
This should display the version number of the pip that was installed.

After completing these steps, Python and pip should be set up on your Ubuntu 22.04 system. You can install any additional Python libraries that you need using pip.

How to set up and use Python virtual environments for Ansible?

Setting up and using Python virtual environments for Ansible can help you manage dependencies for different projects and avoid conflicts between different versions of Python libraries. Here are the steps to set up and use a Python virtual environment for Ansible:

First method
Step 1: Setting up a directory for the virtual environment (recommended): You can set up a directory for the virtual environment by running the following command:
$ mkdir ansible-env

To switch to the ansible-env directory, run:
$ cd ansible-env
OR

```
$ cd !$
```

Step 2: Create a Python virtual environment: To create a new Python virtual environment for Ansible, run the following command:

```
$ python3 -m venv ansible-env
$ ls
```

This will create a new Python virtual environment called "ansible-env" in your current directory.

Step 3: Activate the virtual environment: To activate the virtual environment, run the following command:

```
$ source ansible-env/bin/activate
```

This will activate the virtual environment and make it the default Python environment for your terminal session. You should see the name of your virtual environment in the terminal prompt.

Step 4: Install Ansible and any required dependencies: With the virtual environment activated, you can use pip or python3 to install Ansible and any other required dependencies. For example, you can run the following command to install the latest version of Ansible:

```
$ pip3 install ansible
```

OR

```
$ python3 -m pip install ansible
```

To verify, run:

```
$ which ansible
$ ansible --version
```

Step 5: Use Ansible within the virtual environment: With Ansible and its dependencies installed in the virtual environment, you can use the "ansible" and "ansible-playbook" commands as usual. However, make sure that the virtual environment is activated before running any Ansible commands, by running the following command:

```
$ source ansible-env/bin/activate
```
This will ensure that Ansible uses the correct version of Python and its dependencies.

Step 6: Deactivate the virtual environment: To deactivate the virtual environment, run the following command:
```
$ deactivate
```
This will restore your original Python environment and remove the virtual environment from your terminal session.

Second method
Step 1: Install virtualenv: You can install *virtualenv* by running the following command:
```
$ sudo pip3 install virtualenv
```

Step 2: Create a virtual environment: To create a new virtual environment for Ansible, run the following command:
```
$ virtualenv ansible-env
```
This will create a new directory called "ansible-env" in your current directory and install a new Python environment inside it.

Step 3: Activate the virtual environment: To activate the virtual environment, run the following command:
```
$ source ansible-env/bin/activate
```
This will activate the virtual environment and make it the default Python environment for your terminal session. You should see the name of your virtual environment in the terminal prompt.

Step 4: Install Ansible and any required dependencies: With the virtual environment activated, you can use pip to install Ansible and any other required dependencies. For example, you can run the following command to install the latest version of Ansible:
```
$ pip3 install ansible
```

Step 5: Use Ansible within the virtual environment: With Ansible and its dependencies installed in the virtual environment, you can use the "ansible" and "ansible-playbook" commands as usual. However, make sure that the virtual environment is activated before running any Ansible commands, by running the following command:

`$ source ansible-env/bin/activate`

This will ensure that Ansible uses the correct version of Python and its dependencies.

Step 6: Deactivate the virtual environment: To deactivate the virtual environment, run the following command:

`$ deactivate`

This will restore your original Python environment and remove the virtual environment from your terminal session.

Summary

By using Python virtual environments for Ansible, you can easily manage dependencies and avoid conflicts between different projects or versions of Ansible.

I.III Overview of Ansible architecture and components

An overview of the architecture and components of Ansible!
Ansible's architecture is designed to be simple, scalable, and easy to use. In this section, I will discuss the architecture and components of Ansible.

Architecture of Ansible
Ansible's architecture consists of three main components:
1.   **Control Node:** The Control Node is the machine on which Ansible is installed and executed. It is the machine from which Ansible can manage the infrastructure. The Control Node can be installed on any machine, including a laptop, a desktop, or a server.
2.   **Managed Nodes:** The Managed Nodes are the machines that Ansible manages. These nodes can be physical or virtual machines, and they can be running any operating system, including Linux, macOS, and Windows.
3.   **Ansible Modules:** Ansible Modules are pre-built scripts that are used to perform specific tasks, such as installing packages, configuring files, managing users, and more. Ansible provides a large number of built-in modules, and users can also create their custom modules.

Components of Ansible
Ansible's components include:
1.   **Inventory:** The Inventory is a list of all the Managed Nodes that Ansible can manage. It is a text file that contains a list of IP addresses or hostnames of the Managed Nodes. The Inventory file can be static or dynamic, and it can be stored locally or remotely.
2. **Playbooks:** Playbooks are Ansible's configuration management scripts. They are written in YAML format and define the desired state of the infrastructure. Playbooks contain a set of tasks that

are executed on the Managed Nodes. Playbooks can be used to install packages, configure files, manage users, and more.

3. **Roles:** Roles are a way to organize Playbooks into reusable components. They are a collection of tasks, files, templates, and variables that can be shared across different Playbooks. Roles allow users to create modular and reusable configurations that can be easily maintained and updated.

4. **Ad-hoc Commands:** Ad-hoc commands are used to execute a single task on one or more Managed Nodes. They are run from the command line and do not require a Playbook. Ad-hoc commands are useful for tasks that are not part of a larger configuration management task, such as restarting a service or checking the status of a process.

Conclusion

Ansible's architecture and components are designed to be simple, scalable, and easy to use. Its client-server architecture, inventory, Playbooks, roles, and ad-hoc commands make it a powerful automation tool that can simplify the management of complex IT infrastructure. With its declarative language, Ansible enables users to define the desired state of the infrastructure and automate the necessary tasks to achieve that state.

I.IV Comparison with other automation tools

Automation tools are designed to simplify the management of complex IT infrastructure by automating repetitive tasks and reducing the need for manual intervention. Ansible is one of the most popular automation tools, but other tools offer similar functionality. In this section, I will compare Ansible with other popular automation tools.

Comparison of Ansible with other automation tools

1.   **Puppet:** Puppet is a popular automation tool that uses declarative language to define the desired state of the infrastructure. Like Ansible, Puppet is used to manage large-scale systems and can be used to automate a variety of tasks, such as installing packages, configuring files, and managing users. However, unlike Ansible, Puppet requires a dedicated Puppet Master server, which can be a disadvantage for smaller organizations.

2.   **Chef:** Chef is another popular automation tool that uses declarative language to define the desired state of the infrastructure. Like Ansible and Puppet, Chef is used to manage large-scale systems and can be used to automate a variety of tasks, such as installing packages, configuring files, and managing users. However, Chef has a steeper learning curve than Ansible, making it more challenging for users with less experience.

3.   **SaltStack:** SaltStack is an automation tool that uses a combination of declarative and imperative programming to define the desired state of the infrastructure. Like Ansible, SaltStack can be used to manage large-scale systems and automate various tasks, such as installing packages, configuring files, and managing users. However, SaltStack can be more complex to set up and configure than Ansible, which makes it less accessible to users with less experience.

4. **Terraform:** Terraform is an infrastructure as code (IaC) tool used to provision and manage cloud resources. Unlike Ansible and the other tools mentioned above, Terraform is not designed to manage on-premises infrastructure. Instead, it is used to manage cloud resources, such as virtual machines, storage, and networking. Terraform uses declarative language to define the desired state of the infrastructure, and it can be used to automate the creation and configuration of cloud resources.

Conclusion

In conclusion, Ansible is a powerful automation tool that simplifies the management of complex IT infrastructure. While other automation tools are available, Ansible's simplicity, scalability, and ease of use make it an ideal choice for organizations of all sizes. Using a declarative language and client-server architecture, Ansible enables users to define the desired state of the infrastructure and automate the necessary tasks to achieve that state. Helping organizations improve efficiency, reduce errors, and increase system reliability.

I.V Tips for getting started with Ansible

How to get started with Ansible?

- **Start small**

When getting started with Ansible, it's best to start with small projects and build up your skills gradually. You can start by automating simple tasks such as installing packages, managing files, and running commands on remote servers. As you become more familiar with Ansible, you can move on to more complex tasks, such as deploying applications and managing network infrastructure.

- **Learn YAML syntax**

Ansible uses YAML syntax to define tasks and playbooks. YAML is a human-readable language that uses indentation to define the structure of the data. It's essential to become familiar with YAML syntax when working with Ansible, as it is used extensively throughout the tool.

- **Use Ansible modules**

Ansible modules are pre-built tasks that you can use to automate tasks. There are over 3000 Ansible modules available, covering a wide range of use cases, including system administration, network management, and cloud provisioning. Using modules can help you save time and reduce errors when automating tasks.

- **Use Ansible roles**

Ansible roles are a way to organize and reuse Ansible code. Roles are a collection of tasks, templates, and files that can be easily shared and reused across projects. You can use Roles to define the configuration of a specific component or application, making it easy to manage and maintain complex infrastructures.

- **Use source control**

Using source control, such as Git, helps you manage and track changes to your Ansible code. Source control can help you collaborate with others, manage versions, and ensure that your code is backed up and secure.

- **Test your Ansible code**

Testing is an essential part of any automation project. Ansible provides several tools for testing, including the ansible-lint tool, which can help you identify errors in your code, and the ansible-test tool, which you can use to test your Ansible code against different scenarios.

- **Use Ansible Galaxy**

Ansible Galaxy is a community-driven repository of Ansible roles that you can use to automate tasks. Ansible Galaxy provides a wide range of pre-built roles that can be easily installed and used in your projects. Using Ansible Galaxy can help you save time and improve the reliability of your automation projects.

Conclusion

In conclusion, getting started with Ansible can be challenging. Following the mentioned tips, you can quickly get up to speed and start automating your IT infrastructure. Starting small, learning YAML syntax, using Ansible modules and roles, using source control, testing your code, and using Ansible Galaxy can help you become an Ansible expert in no time.

II. ANSIBLE FUNDAMENTALS

II.I Installing and configuring Ansible

In this section, I will walk through the process of installing and configuring Ansible, an open-source automation tool that can help simplify IT infrastructure management.

Installing Ansible

To install Ansible, you'll need to have a Linux-based system with Python 3 installed. Ansible supports a wide range of Linux distributions, including Ubuntu, CentOS, and Red Hat Enterprise Linux.

How to install Ansible on Debian?

To install Ansible on Debian, you can follow the steps below:

1. To include the official project's PPA (personal package archive) in your system's list of sources, run:

```
$ sudo apt-add-repository ppa:ansible/ansible
```

2. Update the package index and upgrade the system:

```
$ sudo apt update
```

3. Install the dependencies required by Ansible:

```
$ sudo apt install ansible -y
```

4. Verify the installation by checking the version of Ansible:

```
$ ansible --version
```

5. For Ansible to work, you need to ensure that ssh is up and running.

```
$ sudo systemctl status ssh
```

That's it! Ansible should now be installed on your Debian system. You can now proceed with configuring Ansible for your infrastructure management needs.

How to install Ansible on Fedora?

To install Ansible on Fedora, you can follow the steps below:

1. Update the package index and upgrade the system:
```
$ sudo dnf update
```

2. Install Ansible using dnf:
```
$ sudo dnf install -y ansible-core
```

3. Verify the installation by checking the version of Ansible:
```
$ ansible --version
```

4. For Ansible to work, you need to ensure that ssh is up and running.
```
$ sudo systemctl status sshd
```

That's it! Ansible should now be installed on your Fedora system. You can now proceed with configuring Ansible for your infrastructure management needs.

Configuring Ansible

Once you have Ansible installed, you'll need to configure it to work with your infrastructure. The main configuration file for Ansible is called *ansible.cfg*, and it's typically located in the */etc/ansible/* directory.

- */etc/ansible/ansible.cfg* - Config file, used if present.
- *~/.ansible.cfg* - User config file, overrides the default config if present.
- *./ansible.cfg* - Local config file (in current working directory) assumed to be 'project specific' and overrides the rest if present.

Note that
- The *ANSIBLE_CONFIG* environment variable will override all others.

Here are some of the key settings you may want to configure:

- **Inventory**

The inventory file is where you define the hosts that Ansible will manage. By default, Ansible looks for an inventory file at */etc/ansible/hosts*. You can create this file manually and add hosts to it, or you can use a dynamic inventory script that generates the inventory based on your infrastructure.

To edit the contents of your default Ansible inventory on your Ansible control node, run:
$ sudo vim /etc/ansible/hosts

To check your inventory, run:
$ ansible-inventory --list -y

- **SSH settings**

By default, Ansible uses SSH to connect to the hosts in your inventory. You can configure the SSH settings in *ansible.cfg* to specify the username and SSH key to use when connecting to hosts. For example:
[ssh_connection]
ssh_args = -C -o ControlMaster=auto -o ControlPersist=60s
remote_user = myuser

- **Roles path**

Roles are reusable collections of tasks and templates that can be shared across playbooks. By default, Ansible looks for roles in the */etc/ansible/roles/* directory relative to the playbook. You can configure the roles path in *ansible.cfg* to specify a different location for roles. For example:
[defaults]
roles_path = /path/to/roles

Conclusion

Installing and configuring Ansible is relatively straightforward, and once you have it set up, you'll be able to automate many of the routine tasks associated with managing your IT infrastructure. Whether you're deploying applications, managing configuration files, or provisioning new servers, Ansible can help you work more efficiently and effectively. For more information on how to use Ansible, check out the official documentation or join the Ansible community.

II.II Creating a test environment

Before you can run your playbooks on your production environment, it's important to test them in a development or staging environment. This ensures that your playbooks work as expected and that they won't cause any issues in your production environment. In this section, I'll walk you through the process of creating an Ansible test environment.

Requirements
Before we get started, make sure you have the following requirements:

- A virtualization software (e.g., VirtualBox or VMware)
- A Linux distribution (e.g., RHEL, Ubuntu)
- Ansible installed on your local machine

Creating a simple test environment!
One VM only

Step 1: Set up a virtual machine
The first step in creating an Ansible test environment is to set up a virtual machine (VM). You can use virtualization software like VirtualBox or VMware to create a new VM. When setting up the VM, make sure to install a Linux distribution, such as RHEL or Ubuntu.

Step 2: Configure SSH access
Once your VM is up and running, you'll need to configure SSH access to the VM. This will allow you to run Ansible playbooks on the VM. To do this, open a terminal on your local machine and run the following command:
`$ ssh-copy-id username@vm-ip-address`
Replace "username" with the username you use to log in to your VM and "vm-ip-address" with the IP address of your VM.

Step 3: Create an inventory file
An inventory file is a list of hosts that Ansible can connect to and run playbooks on. To create an inventory file, open a new file in your favorite text editor and enter the IP address of your VM:
[web-servers]
vm-ip-address
Save the file as "inventory" in your local machine's working directory.

Step 4: Write a playbook
Now it's time to write a simple playbook to test your environment. Open a new file in your text editor and enter the following:

YAML

```yaml
---
- hosts: web-servers
  tasks:
  - name: Ping test
    ping:
```
Save the file as "ping.yml" in your local machine's working directory.

Step 5: Run the playbook
To run the playbook, open a terminal on your local machine and navigate to your working directory. Then run the following command:
```
$ ansible-playbook -i inventory ping.yml
```
This command tells Ansible to run the "ping.yml" playbook on the hosts listed in the "inventory" file.

Conclusion
Creating an Ansible test environment is a straightforward process. By following the steps outlined in this section, you can set up a simple Ansible test environment that you can use to test your playbooks before running them in production. Remember to

always test your playbooks before running them in a production environment to ensure that they work as expected and don't cause any issues.

Creating an advanced test environment!
Three VMs:
- One control node
- Two managed nodes

Ansible is based on Python and uses SSH to control managed nodes through the control node. You need to install Ansible on the control node and ensure that OpenSSH and Python are running on both the control node and the managed nodes. You do not need to install Ansible on managed nodes.

Step 1: Set up a virtual machine
The first step in creating an Ansible test environment is to set up a virtual machine (VM). You can use virtualization software like VirtualBox or VMware to create a new VM. When setting up the VM, make sure to install a Linux distribution, such as RHEL or Ubuntu.

Step 2: Install Ansible on the control node
1. Update the package index and upgrade the system:
`$ sudo dnf update`

2. Install Ansible using dnf:
`$ sudo dnf install -y ansible-core`

3. Verify the installation by checking the version of Ansible:
`$ ansible --version`

Step 3: Check the sshd service status
1. For Ansible to work, you need to ensure that the *sshd* service is up and running on all VMs.
`$ sudo systemctl status sshd`

2. To check the ssh status in firewall, run:
$ sudo firewall-cmd --list-all

3. To enable ssh service in firewall public zone, run:
$ sudo firewall-cmd --add-service=ssh --zone=public --permanent
$ sudo firewall-cmd --reload

4. To verify, run:
$ sudo firewall-cmd --list-all

Step 4: Create an Ansible user
Instead of using the root user (Not recommended), you need to create an Ansible user with sudo privileges on all VMs:
1. To create the new user, run the following command on all nodes:
useradd -m ansadmin

2. Set *ansadmin* password on all nodes by using the command:
passwd ansadmin

3. To grant the user *ansadmin* sudo privileges on all nodes, run:
echo "ansadmin ALL=(ALL) NOPASSWD:ALL" >> /etc/sudoers
OR
echo "ansadmin ALL=(ALL) NOPASSWD:ALL" > /etc/sudoers.d/ansadmin

4. Login as user *ansadmin* on the control node by running the following command:
$ su - ansadmin

5. To generate the authentication key, run:
$ ssh-keygen

Step 5: Configure SSH access
Once your VM is up and running, you'll need to configure SSH access to the managed VMs. This will allow you to run Ansible playbooks on them.
1. To do this, copy the user *ansadmin* public ssh key to all managed

nodes by using the command:
```
$ ssh-copy-id managed_node_x
```

2. To verify, run:
```
$ ssh managed_node_x
```

Step 6: Create an Ansible directory in the user's home directory
1. To create `ansible` directory in the user's home directory, run:
```
$ sudo mkdir ~/ansible
```

Step 7: Create an inventory file
An inventory file is a list of hosts that Ansible can connect to and run playbooks on.
1. To create an inventory file, open a new file in your favorite text editor:
```
$ sudo nano ~/ansible/inventory
```

2. Enter the IP address of the managed nodes:
```
[web-servers]
managed_node_1
managed_node_2
```

3. Save and quit.

Step 8: Write a playbook
Now it's time to write a simple playbook to test your environment.
1. Create a `playbook` directory in the `ansible` directory:
```
$ sudo mkdir ~/ansible/playbooks
```

1. Open a new file in your text editor:
```
$ sudo nano ~/ansible/playbooks/ping.yml
```

2. Enter the following:
```
---
- hosts: web-servers
  tasks:
  - name: Ping test
    ping:
```

3. Save the file as "ping.yml" in your control machine's working directory.

Step 9: Create an Ansible Configuration File (`ansible.cfg`)
To create an Ansible configuration file (`ansible.cfg`) with the specified settings on RHEL 9, follow these steps:

1. Open a Terminal

Open a terminal window on your RHEL 9 machine.

2. Navigate to the Desired Directory

In this case, you want to create the `ansible.cfg` file at `/home/ansadmin/ansible/`. You can navigate to this directory using the `cd` command. For example:

```
$ cd ~/ansible/
```

3. Create the Configuration File

Now, you can create the `ansible.cfg` file using a text editor like `nano` or `vim`. For simplicity, I'll use `nano` in this example. You can install `nano` if it's not already installed:

```
$ sudo dnf install nano -y
```

Then, create the configuration file:

```
$ nano ansible.cfg
```

4. Add Configuration Settings

Inside the `nano` editor, add the following configuration settings:

```
[defaults]
roles_path = ~/ansible/roles
inventory = ~/ansible/inventory
remote_user = ansadmin
```

`forks = 10`

Explanation of settings:

- `roles_path`: This setting defines the path where Ansible will look for roles. In this case, it's set to `~/ansible/roles`.

- `inventory`: This setting specifies the path to the inventory file that Ansible should use. It's set to `~/ansible/inventory`.

- `remote_user`: This sets the default remote user that Ansible will use when connecting to remote hosts. It's set to `ansadmin`.

- `forks`: This sets the maximum number of parallel processes or "forks" that Ansible will use when executing tasks. It's set to `10`.

5. Save and Exit

To save the changes in `nano`, press `Ctrl+O`, then press `Enter`. To exit `nano`, press `Ctrl+X`.

6. Verify the Configuration File

You can verify that the `ansible.cfg` file was created correctly by listing the contents of the directory:
`$ ls`
You should see the `ansible.cfg` file listed.

Step 10: Run the playbook
To run the playbook, open a terminal on your local machine and navigate to your working directory. Then run the following command:
`$ ansible-playbook -i ~/ansible/inventory ~/ansible/playbooks/ping.yml`
This command tells Ansible to run the "ping.yml" playbook on the hosts listed in the "inventory" file.

II.III Ansible Ad-Hoc Commands

One of the key features of Ansible is its ability to execute ad-hoc commands on remote hosts. Ad-hoc commands allow administrators to quickly perform one-time tasks or tests on a specific host or group of hosts without having to create a playbook or task list. In this section, I will explore Ansible ad-hoc commands and how they can be used to manage and configure remote hosts.

What are Ansible Ad-Hoc Commands?
Ad-hoc commands are one-off commands that are executed directly from the command line using the **ansible** command. Ad-hoc commands are a quick and easy way to perform simple tasks or tests on one or more remote hosts without having to create a playbook or task list.
Ad-hoc commands are particularly useful for system administrators who need to perform quick checks or tests, such as checking the disk usage on a remote host or testing connectivity to a specific port.

Here's an example of an ad-hoc command that lists all the files in the /etc directory on a remote host:
`$ ansible all -i inventory.ini -m shell -a 'ls /etc'`
Let's break down this command:

- **ansible all** - The **ansible** command is used to execute the ad-hoc command, and **all** specifies that the command should be executed on all hosts in the inventory.
- **-i inventory.ini** - This option specifies the inventory file to use for the command. The inventory file is a list of all the hosts that Ansible can manage, along with their connection details.
- **-m shell** - This option specifies the Ansible module to use for the command. In this case, we're using the **shell** module, which allows us to execute a shell command on

the remote host.

- **-a 'ls /etc'** - This option specifies the arguments to pass to the module. In this case, we're passing the **ls /etc** command, which lists all the files in the **/etc** directory on the remote host.

Common Uses of Ansible Ad-Hoc Commands

Here are some common use cases for Ansible ad-hoc commands:

- **Checking Disk Usage**

One of the most common tasks for system administrators is monitoring disk usage on their servers. Here's an example of an ad-hoc command that checks the disk usage on a remote host:

$ ansible all -i inventory.ini -m shell -a 'df -h'

This command uses the **df** command to show the disk usage on the remote host.

- **Restarting a Service**

Sometimes, you may need to restart a service on a remote host. Here's an example of an ad-hoc command that restarts the Apache service on a remote host:

$ ansible webservers -i inventory.ini -m service -a 'name=httpd state=restarted'

This command uses the **service** module to restart the Apache service on the **webservers** group of hosts.

- **Installing a Package**

Another common task is installing packages on remote hosts. Here's an example of an ad-hoc command that installs the **git** package on a remote host:

$ ansible webservers -i inventory.ini -m yum -a 'name=git state=installed'

This command uses the **yum** module to install the **git** package on the **webservers** group of hosts.

- **Copying Files**

You can also use ad-hoc commands to copy files from the control node to remote hosts. Here's an example of an ad-hoc command that copies a file from the previous paragraph:

$ ansible webservers -i inventory.ini -m copy -a 'src=/path/to/

`local/file dest=/path/to/remote/file'`

This command uses the **copy** module to copy a file from the control node to the **webservers** group of hosts.

Conclusion

Ansible ad-hoc commands are a powerful tool that allows system administrators to quickly perform simple tasks or tests on remote hosts without having to create a playbook or task list. Ad-hoc commands can be used for a variety of tasks, such as checking disk usage, restarting services, installing packages, and copying files.

When using ad-hoc commands, it's important to remember that they are not a replacement for Ansible playbooks or task lists. Ad-hoc commands are best used for one-time tasks or tests, while playbooks and task lists should be used for more complex and repetitive tasks.

As you're new to Ansible, ad-hoc commands are a great way to get started and familiarize yourself with the tool. With practice and experience, you'll soon be able to use Ansible to automate and manage your entire infrastructure.

II.IV YAML Overview

What is YAML?
YAML (short for "YAML Ain't Markup Language") is a human-readable data serialization format that is often used in Ansible playbooks to define tasks, variables, and other configuration data. In this section, I'll cover the basics of YAML syntax and how to use it effectively in Ansible.

YAML Syntax
YAML uses indentation to indicate structure, similar to Python. Here's an example YAML file:

YAML

```
---
# This is a comment
servers:
 - name: webserver1
   ip: 10.0.0.1
   os: Ubuntu 22.04
 - name: webserver2
   ip: 10.0.0.2
   os: CentOS 8
```

In this example, I have a list of servers, each represented as a dictionary with three keys: *name*, *ip*, and *os*. Notice that the servers list is indented two spaces to the right of the --- marker at the top of the file. Each server in the list is indented another two spaces to the right.

Here are some other important things to keep in mind when working with YAML:
  - YAML is case-sensitive. Be sure to use the correct capitalization for keywords, variables, and other elements.
  - YAML uses colons to separate keys from values, and

commas to separate items in a list.
- YAML supports strings, numbers, booleans, null, and other data types.
- YAML uses hashes (#) for comments.

YAML in Ansible Playbooks

In Ansible playbooks, YAML is used to define tasks, variables, and other configuration data. Here's an example playbook that installs the *nginx* package on a group of web servers:

YAML

```
---
- name: Install Nginx
  hosts: webservers
  become: true
  tasks:
    - name: Install Nginx package
      apt:
        name: nginx
        state: present
```

In this playbook, I have a single task that installs the *nginx* package using the *apt* module. Notice that each task is indented two spaces to the right of the tasks keyword and that the *name*, *hosts*, and *become* keywords are indented one level higher.

Here are a few more examples of YAML syntax in Ansible:

Defining variables:

YAML

```
---
my_variable: some_value
another_variable: 123
```

Using conditionals:

YAML

```yaml
---
- name: Check disk space
  hosts: webservers
  become: true
  tasks:
    - name: Check free space on root partition
      shell: df -h /
      register: disk_space
    - name: Send email if disk space is low
      mail:
        to: admin@example.com
        subject: "Low disk space on {{ inventory_hostname }}"
        body: "Only {{ disk_space.stdout_lines[1].split()[3] }} free on {{ inventory_hostname }}"
      when: disk_space.stdout_lines[1].split()[3] | int < 10
```

Using loops:

YAML

```yaml
---
- name: Install multiple packages
  hosts: webservers
  become: true
  vars:
    packages:
      - nginx
      - postgresql
      - redis-server
  tasks:
    - name: Install packages
      apt:
        name: "{{ item }}"
        state: present
      loop: "{{ packages }}"
```

Using templates:

YAML

```
---
- name: Create configuration file
  hosts: webservers
  become: true
  tasks:
   - name: Copy template file
     template:
       src: myapp.conf.j2
       dest: /etc/myapp.conf
```

In this example, I'm using the template module to copy a *Jinja2* template file (*myapp.conf.j2*) to the remote host, rendering it with variables and writing the resulting file to */etc/myapp.conf*.

Conclusion

YAML is a powerful and flexible data serialization format that is well-suited for use in Ansible playbooks. With its intuitive syntax and support for complex data structures, it's a great tool for defining tasks, variables, and other configuration data in a human-readable and easy-to-maintain way. I hope this section has helped you get started with YAML in Ansible!

II.V Creating and managing inventory files

In this section, I will walk through the process of creating and managing inventory files on Ansible, an open-source automation tool that can help simplify IT infrastructure management.

What is an inventory file?
An inventory file in Ansible is a list of the hosts and groups that Ansible will manage. It's a simple text file that contains the IP addresses or hostnames of the machines that you want to manage, as well as any relevant information such as usernames, passwords, and SSH keys.
An inventory file can be static or dynamic. A static inventory file is a list of hosts that don't change, while a dynamic inventory file is generated on the fly based on some external data source such as an API or a database.

Creating a static inventory file
To create a static inventory file, you can create a new file in the */etc/ansible/hosts* directory. For example, to create a file called *myhosts* that contains a list of hosts, you can run the following command:
$ sudo nano /etc/ansible/hosts/myhosts

In this file, you can define the hosts and groups that Ansible will manage. Here's an example inventory file that defines two hosts, Ib1 and Ib2, and two groups, Ibservers, and databases:
[Ibservers]
Ib1
Ib2

[databases]
db1
db2

In this example, the Ibservers group contains the hosts Ib1 and Ib2, while the databases group contains the hosts db1 and db2. You can also define variables for individual hosts or groups in the inventory file:

[Ibservers]
Ib1   ansible_ssh_user=myuser
ansible_ssh_private_key_file=~/.ssh/id_rsa
Ib2   ansible_ssh_user=myuser
ansible_ssh_private_key_file=~/.ssh/id_rsa

[databases]
db1   ansible_ssh_user=myuser
ansible_ssh_private_key_file=~/.ssh/id_rsa
db2   ansible_ssh_user=myuser
ansible_ssh_private_key_file=~/.ssh/id_rsa

In this example, I've defined the *ansible_ssh_user* and *ansible_ssh_private_key_file* variables for each host. These variables specify the SSH username and private key file to use when connecting to each host.

Creating a dynamic inventory file

To create a dynamic inventory file, you can write a script that generates the inventory based on some external data source. For example, you could write a script that queries a cloud provider's API and generates an inventory file based on the list of instances.

There are many pre built dynamic inventory scripts available for Ansible, which can be found in the */usr/share/ansible/inventory* directory. For example, there are dynamic inventory scripts for Amazon EC2, Google Cloud Platform, and Microsoft Azure.

To use a dynamic inventory script, you'll need to specify it in your *ansible.cfg* configuration file. For example, to use the Amazon EC2 dynamic inventory script, you can add the following to your *ansible.cfg* file:

[defaults]
inventory = /usr/share/ansible/inventory/ec2.py

Conclusion

Creating and managing inventory files is a crucial part of using Ansible to manage your IT infrastructure. Whether you're using a static inventory file or a dynamic inventory script, your inventory file should accurately reflect the hosts and groups that Ansible will manage. By properly configuring your inventory file, you'll be able to effectively automate tasks across your infrastructure. For more information on how to use Ansible, check out the official documentation or join the Ansible community.

II.VI Writing and executing playbooks

Writing and executing playbooks is a fundamental aspect of automating tasks in infrastructure management. Playbooks are used in Ansible, an open-source automation tool, to define the tasks that need to be executed on remote machines. In this section, I will cover the basics of writing and executing playbooks.

What is a playbook?
A playbook is a YAML file that contains a series of tasks to be executed by Ansible. Each task is defined as a dictionary with key-value pairs that specify the name of the task, the module to be used, and the arguments to be passed to the module. Playbooks can be used for a wide range of tasks, from deploying applications to configuring servers.

Writing a playbook
When writing a playbook, the first step is to define the hosts on which the playbook will be executed. This can be done by specifying the hosts in the inventory file or by using the "hosts" keyword in the playbook itself. Once the hosts have been defined, the tasks can be defined using the "tasks" keyword.

Each task in the playbook should have a unique name, which will be used to identify it in the output. The module to be used should also be specified, along with any arguments that need to be passed to the module. Here is an example of a simple playbook that installs the Apache Ib server on a remote machine:

YAML

```
---
- hosts: Ibserver
  tasks:
  - name: Install Apache
    apt:
```

```
  name: apache2
  state: present
```

In this example, the "hosts" keyword is used to specify the target host, which is called "Ibserver". The "tasks" keyword is used to define the tasks that need to be executed. The task is called "Install Apache" and uses the "apt" module to install the Apache Ib server package.

Executing a playbook

To execute a playbook, use the "ansible-playbook" command followed by the name of the playbook file. Here is an example of how to execute the playbook I defined earlier:

```
$ ansible-playbook install_apache.yml
```

This will execute the "install_apache.yml" playbook on all the hosts defined in the inventory file or in the playbook itself.

Conclusion

Playbooks are a powerful tool for automating tasks in infrastructure management. They allow you to define tasks simply and intuitively and execute them on remote machines with ease. By following the guidelines outlined in this section, you should be able to write and execute playbooks effectively and efficiently.

II.VII Managing variables and facts

Managing variables and facts is a crucial aspect of working with Ansible, an open-source automation tool used for infrastructure management. In this section, I will cover the basics of managing variables and facts in Ansible.

What are variables and facts?

Variables and facts are used in Ansible to store data that is used to configure and manage remote systems. Variables are user-defined and can be used to store information such as IP addresses, hostnames, and other configuration data. Facts, on the other hand, are pieces of information that Ansible collects from the remote system, such as the hostname, IP address, and operating system version.

Defining variables

Variables can be defined in several places, including the inventory file, playbook, or a separate file. The most common method is to define variables in the playbook itself. Here's an example of how to define a variable in a playbook:

YAML

```
---
- hosts: Ibserver
 vars:
   apache_port: 80
 tasks:
 - name: Configure Apache
   template:
     src: /etc/httpd/conf/httpd.conf.j2
     dest: /etc/httpd/conf/httpd.conf
   notify: restart apache
```

In this example, the "vars" keyword is used to define a variable called "apache_port" with a value of 80. The variable can then be used in the playbook by enclosing it in double curly braces, like this: {{ apache_port }}.

Using facts

Facts are collected by Ansible automatically when a task is executed on a remote system. Facts are stored in a dictionary and can be accessed in the playbook using the "ansible_facts" variable. Here's an example of how to use facts in a playbook:

YAML

```yaml
---
- hosts: Ibserver
  tasks:
  - name: Display hostname
    debug:
      msg: "Hostname is {{ ansible_facts['hostname'] }}"
```

In this example, the "debug" module is used to display the hostname of the remote system. The "ansible_facts" variable is used to access the facts dictionary, and the "hostname" key is used to retrieve the hostname of the remote system.

Overriding variables

Variables can be overridden in several ways, including in the inventory file, command line, or playbook. The most common method is to override variables in the playbook itself using the "vars_prompt" keyword. Here's an example of how to override a variable in a playbook:

YAML

```yaml
---
- hosts: Ibserver
  vars_prompt:
  - name: apache_port
    prompt: "Enter Apache port number"
    default: "80"
```

```
tasks:
- name: Configure Apache
  template:
    src: /etc/httpd/conf/httpd.conf.j2
    dest: /etc/httpd/conf/httpd.conf
  notify: restart apache
```

In this example, the "vars_prompt" keyword is used to prompt the user to enter a value for the "apache_port" variable. If the user does not enter a value, the default value of 80 will be used.

Conclusion

Variables and facts are essential tools for managing and configuring remote systems in Ansible. By following the guidelines outlined in this section, you should be able to manage variables and facts effectively and efficiently. Understanding how to use and override variables and facts is crucial to creating effective and efficient automation scripts.

II.VIII Debugging and error handling

Debugging and error handling are crucial aspects of working with Ansible, an open-source automation tool used for infrastructure management. In this section, I will cover the basics of debugging and error handling in Ansible.

Debugging in Ansible
Debugging is the process of identifying and fixing errors or problems in your automation scripts. Ansible provides several tools for debugging, including the "debug" module, which allows you to print out information during the execution of your playbook.

Here's an example of how to use the "debug" module to print out a variable value:

YAML

```
---
- hosts: Ibserver
  vars:
    apache_port: 80
  tasks:
  - name: Debugging with Ansible
    debug:
      var: apache_port
```

In this example, the "debug" module is used to print out the value of the "apache_port" variable. The "var" keyword is used to specify the variable to print.

In addition to the "debug" module, Ansible provides several other modules for debugging, including "assert" and "fail". The "assert" module allows you to test for a condition and fail the task if the condition is not met. The "fail" module allows you to fail a task with a custom error message.

Error Handling in Ansible

Error handling is the process of dealing with errors or exceptions that occur during the execution of your automation scripts. Ansible provides several tools for error handling, including the "failed_when" keyword, which allows you to control when a task should fail.

Here's an example of how to use the "failed_when" keyword to control when a task should fail:

YAML

```
---
- hosts: Ibserver
  tasks:
  - name: Execute a command
    command: /bin/false
    register: result
    failed_when: result.rc != 0
```

In this example, the "command" module is used to execute a command that will always fail. The "register" keyword is used to store the result of the command in a variable called "result". The "failed_when" keyword is used to specify that the task should fail if the return code of the command is not equal to 0.

In addition to the "failed_when" keyword, Ansible provides several other keywords for error handling, including "ignore_errors", which allows you to ignore errors and continue with the execution of your playbook.

Conclusion

Debugging and error handling are essential tools for managing and configuring remote systems in Ansible. By following the guidelines outlined in this section, you should be able to debug and handle errors effectively and efficiently. Understanding how to use and override variables and facts is crucial to creating effective and efficient automation scripts. With the right tools and knowledge, you can create automation scripts that are reliable and efficient.

III. ADVANCED PLAYBOOK FEATURES

III.I Using conditionals and loops in Ansible.

Ansible is a powerful automation tool that allows you to manage and configure multiple servers and network devices with ease. It uses a YAML-based language to define tasks, which can be executed on one or more remote hosts. In this section, I'll focus on how to use conditionals and loops in Ansible to create more complex playbooks.

Conditionals in Ansible

Conditionals are used in Ansible to execute a task only if a certain condition is met. The most common type of conditional in Ansible is the "when" statement. This statement allows you to specify a condition that must be true for the task to be executed. Here's an example:

YAML

```
- name: Install Apache if it's not already installed
  apt:
    name: apache2
    state: present
        when:    ansible_distribution    ==    "Ubuntu"    and
ansible_distribution_release == "22.04"
```

In this example, the "apt" module is used to install Apache on an Ubuntu 22.04 server. The "when" statement checks if the distribution is Ubuntu 22.04 before executing the task. If the condition is not met, the task is skipped.

You can also use the "failed_when" statement to specify a condition that must be true for the task to fail. For example:

YAML

```
- name: Check if a file exists
```

```
stat:
  path: /path/to/file
register: file_info
failed_when: file_info.stat.exists == false
```

In this example, the "stat" module is used to check if a file exists. The "register" statement saves the result of the task to a variable called "file_info". The "failed_when" statement specifies that the task should fail if the file does not exist.

Loops in Ansible

Loops in Ansible are used to iterate a task multiple times with different values. The most common type of loop in Ansible is the "with_items" statement. This statement allows you to specify a list of items for which the task should be executed. This is an example:

YAML

```
- name: Install multiple packages
  apt:
    name: "{{ item }}"
    state: present
  with_items:
    - apache2
    - mysql-server
    - php7.0
```

In this example, the "apt" module is used to install multiple packages on a server. The "with_items" statement specifies a list of package names that the task should be executed for.

You can also use the "loop" statement to loop over a list of items. Here's an example:

YAML

```
- name: Create multiple users
  user:
```

```yaml
  name: "{{ item }}"
  state: present
loop:
 - alice
 - bob
 - charlie
```

In this example, the "user" module is used to create multiple users on a server. The "loop" statement specifies a list of user names that the task should be executed for.

Combining conditionals and loops

You can combine conditionals and loops in Ansible to create more complex playbooks. Here's an example:

YAML

```yaml
- name: Install Apache if it's not already installed
  apt:
   name: apache2
   state: present
       when:    ansible_distribution    ==    "Ubuntu"   and
ansible_distribution_release == "22.04"

- name: Configure Apache virtual hosts
  template:
   src: virtualhost.j2
   dest: /etc/apache2/sites-available/{{ item.domain }}
  when: item.ssl == true
  loop:
   - { domain: example.com, ssl: true }
```

III.II Handling errors and exceptions in Ansible.

Ansible is a powerful automation tool that allows you to manage and configure multiple servers and network devices with ease. In this section, I'll focus on how to handle errors and exceptions in Ansible to create more robust and reliable playbooks.

Error handling in Ansible

Error handling in Ansible is done using the "failed" module. This module is used to mark a task as failed and exit the playbook. Here's an example:

YAML

```
- name: Check if a file exists
  stat:
   path: /path/to/file
  register: file_info

- name: Print an error message if the file doesn't exist
  debug:
   msg: "The file does not exist"
  when: file_info.stat.exists == false
  failed: true
```

In this example, the "stat" module is used to check if a file exists. The "register" statement saves the result of the task to a variable called "file_info". The "debug" statement prints an error message if the file does not exist. The "when" statement checks if the file does not exist, and the "failed" statement marks the task as failed.

You can also use the "ignore_errors" statement to ignore errors and continue executing the playbook. Here's an example:

YAML

```yaml
- name: Stop and disable the Apache service
  systemd:
    name: apache2.service
    state: stopped
    enabled: false
  ignore_errors: true
```

In this example, the "systemd" module is used to stop and disable the Apache service. The "ignore_errors" statement ignores any errors that may occur and continues executing the playbook.

Exception handling in Ansible

Exception handling in Ansible is done using the "block" module. This module allows you to group a set of tasks and handle any exceptions that may occur. Here's an example:

YAML

```yaml
- name: Stop and disable the Apache service
  block:
    - name: Stop the Apache service
      systemd:
        name: apache2.service
        state: stopped
    - name: Disable the Apache service
      systemd:
        name: apache2.service
        enabled: false
  rescue:
    - name: Print an error message
      debug:
        msg: "An error occurred while stopping or disabling the Apache service"
```

In this example, the "block" module is used to group the tasks for stopping and disabling the Apache service. The "rescue" statement is used to handle any exceptions that may occur. If an error occurs, the "rescue" statement executes the tasks in the block and prints an error message.

You can also use the "always" statement to execute a set of tasks regardless of whether an exception occurs or not. Here's an example:

YAML

```
- name: Stop and disable the Apache service
  block:
   - name: Stop the Apache service
     systemd:
       name: apache2.service
       state: stopped
   - name: Disable the Apache service
     systemd:
       name: apache2.service
       enabled: false
  rescue:
   - name: Print an error message
     debug:
       msg: "An error occurred while stopping or disabling the Apache
service"
  always:
   - name: Restart the Apache service
     systemd:
       name: apache2.service
       state: started
```

In this example, the "always" statement is used to restart the Apache service regardless of whether an exception occurs or not.

Conclusion

Handling errors and exceptions in Ansible is essential for creating robust and reliable playbooks. The "failed" module is used to mark

III.III Creating and using templates

What are templates in Ansible?
Templates are files that can be used to create dynamic content. They are created using a template engine, which allows you to use variables and loops to generate the content. In Ansible, the Jinja2 template engine is used to create templates.

Creating a template in Ansible
To create a template in Ansible, you first need to create a file with the template content. The file should have the ".j2" extension to indicate that it is a Jinja2 template. Here's an example:

```
# template.j2
Hello {{ name }}!
```

```
{% for item in items %}
- {{ item }}
{% endfor %}
```

In this example, the template includes a variable called "name" and a loop that iterates over a list called "items".

Using a template in Ansible
To use a template in Ansible, you need to create a task that copies the template to the destination server. Here's an example:

YAML

```
- name: Copy a template to a remote server
  template:
    src: template.j2
    dest: /path/to/file
    vars:
      name: John
      items:
        - Apple
        - Banana
```

- Orange

In this example, the "template" module is used to copy the template to the destination server. The "src" parameter specifies the path to the template file, and the "dest" parameter specifies the path to the destination file on the remote server. The "vars" parameter is used to specify the variables that will be used in the template. In this case, the "name" variable is set to "John" and the "items" list is set to ["Apple", "Banana", "Orange"].

When the task is executed, the template is rendered with the specified variables and copied to the destination server.

Using variables in templates
Templates in Ansible can also use variables defined in inventory or group variables files. Here's an example:

```
# template.j2
Hello {{ name }} from {{ location }}!

{% for item in items %}
- {{ item }}
{% endfor %}
makefile

# inventory file
[Ib]
server1 ansible_host=192.168.1.1

[Ib:vars]
name=John
location=New York
items=["Apple", "Banana", "Orange"]

# playbook
- name: Copy a template to a remote server
  template:
    src: template.j2
    dest: /path/to/file
```

In this example, the "inventory" file defines variables for the "Ib" group. The "playbook" does not specify any variables for the "template" task, so the variables defined in the inventory file will be used.

When the task is executed, the template is rendered with the variables defined in the inventory file and copied to the destination server.

Conclusion

Templates in Ansible are a powerful way to create dynamic content that can be customized based on variables and loops. By using templates, you can create reusable and flexible playbooks that can be adapted to different environments and use cases.

III.IV Working with Ansible roles

Ansible is a popular configuration management tool that allows you to automate IT infrastructure provisioning, configuration management, and application deployment. One of the key features of Ansible is its support for roles, which allows you to organize and reuse your playbooks and tasks in a modular fashion. In this section, I will explore what Ansible roles are, how to create and use them, and some best practices to follow when working with Ansible roles.

What are Ansible's roles?

In Ansible, roles are a way to group related tasks, variables, and files in a structured manner. A role is a self-contained unit of configuration that can be reused across multiple playbooks. Roles are defined in a directory structure that follows a specific convention, and they can contain the following components:

1. **Tasks:** These are the instructions that Ansible executes to carry out a particular action.
2. **Handlers:** These are the tasks that are triggered by an event, such as a change in a configuration file.
3. **Templates:** These are files that contain configuration data and can be customized for each deployment.
4. Variables: These are the values that Ansible uses to configure the system.
5. **Files:** These are static files that are copied to the remote system during deployment.
6. **Meta:** This file contains metadata about the role, such as its dependencies and author.

Creating an Ansible role

To create an Ansible role, you need to follow a specific directory structure. The structure of an Ansible role looks like this:

myrole/

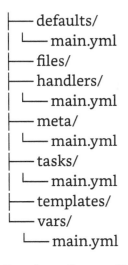

```
├── defaults/
│   └── main.yml
├── files/
├── handlers/
│   └── main.yml
├── meta/
│   └── main.yml
├── tasks/
│   └── main.yml
├── templates/
└── vars/
    └── main.yml
```

In the above directory structure, each subdirectory has a specific purpose:

- **defaults:** This directory contains the default variables for the role.
- **files:** This directory contains static files that will be copied to the remote system.
- **handlers:** This directory contains handlers, which are triggered by events such as configuration changes.
- **meta:** This directory contains metadata about the role, such as its author and dependencies.
- **tasks:** This directory contains the tasks that will be executed by Ansible.
- **templates:** This directory contains configuration files that can be customized for each deployment.
- **vars:** This directory contains variables that will be used to configure the system.

Note that

- The Ansible role has a defined directory structure with eight main standard directories. You must include at least one of these directories per role. You can delete any directories that are not used by the role.

Best practices for working with Ansible roles

Here are some best practices to follow when working with Ansible roles:

1. **Use roles to organize your playbook:** Roles are a great way to break down your playbook into smaller, more manageable chunks. This makes your playbook easier to understand and maintain.

2. **Use role dependencies:** Roles can depend on other roles. Use this feature to reduce duplication of effort and improve the reusability of your code.

3. **Use defaults to set sane defaults:** Defaults are a great way to set sensible default values for your variables. Use them to avoid duplication of effort and reduce the amount of configuration you need to do.

4. **Use variables sparingly:** Variables are a great way to make your playbook flexible and reusable. However, overusing variables can make your playbook difficult to understand and maintain.

5. **Use the include_role module to include roles in other roles:** The *include_role* module allows you to include a role in another role. This is useful when you need to reuse a role in multiple places.

Conclusion

In conclusion, Ansible roles are a powerful way to organize and reuse your Ansible playbooks. They allow you to break down your playbook into

III.V Creating and using
Ansible collections

Ansible collections are a powerful way to package and distribute your Ansible content, including modules, plugins, playbooks, and roles. Collections provide a modular and flexible way to extend Ansible's functionality beyond its built-in modules and plugins. In this section, I will explore what Ansible collections are, how to create and use them, and some best practices to follow when working with Ansible collections.

What are Ansible collections?

Ansible collections are a way to package and distribute Ansible content, including modules, plugins, playbooks, and roles. Collections provide a modular and flexible way to extend Ansible's functionality beyond its built-in modules and plugins. Collections are designed to be versioned and can be installed and managed using the ansible-galaxy command-line tool.

Creating an Ansible collection

To create an Ansible collection, you need to follow a specific directory structure. The structure of an Ansible collection looks like this:

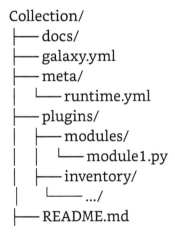

```
Collection/
├── docs/
├── galaxy.yml
├── meta/
│   └── runtime.yml
├── plugins/
│   ├── modules/
│   │   └── module1.py
│   ├── inventory/
│   │   └── .../
├── README.md
```

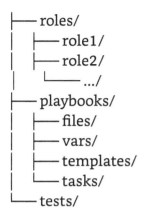

```
├── roles/
│   ├── role1/
│   ├── role2/
│   └── .../
├── playbooks/
│   ├── files/
│   ├── vars/
│   ├── templates/
│   └── tasks/
└── tests/
```

In the above directory structure, each subdirectory has a specific purpose:

- **galaxy.yml:** This file contains metadata about the collection, such as its name, version, and dependencies.
- **plugins:** This directory contains custom plugins that are used by the collection.
- roles: This directory contains roles that are part of the collection.
- **README.md:** This file contains documentation about the collection.

Using an Ansible collection

To use an Ansible collection, you need to install it using the `ansible-galaxy` command-line tool. You can install a collection from Ansible Galaxy, a private repository, or a local file system. Once installed, you can use the collection in your playbook by specifying its name in the roles section of your playbook.

Note that

- A Collection is a simple data structure. None of the directories is required unless you have specific content belonging to one of them. A collection requires a *galaxy.yml* file at the group root level. This file contains all the metadata that Galaxy and other tools need to package, build, and publish the collection.
- Ansible only accepts *.md* extensions for the *README* file

and any files in the /docs folder.

Here is an example of using a collection in a playbook:

YAML

```
- name: My playbook
  hosts: all
  roles:
   - my_collection.my_role_1
   - my_collection.my_role_2
```

Best practices for working with Ansible collections

Here are some best practices to follow when working with Ansible collections:

- **Use collections to modularize your content:** Collections are a great way to modularize your content and make it easier to reuse and share. Use collections to package related modules, plugins, playbooks, and roles.
- **Use clear naming conventions for your collections:** Use a clear and consistent naming convention for your collections to make it easy for others to find and use them.
- **Use semantic versioning for your collections:** Use semantic versioning to version your collections. This makes it clear what has changed between versions and allows users to choose the version that best suits their needs.
- **Document your collections:** Document your collections to make it easy for others to understand how to use them.
- **Test your collections:** Test your collections to ensure that they work as expected and are compatible with the versions of Ansible that you

IV. INFRASTRUCTURE AUTOMATION

IV.I Managing system configurations with Ansible

Ansible is a popular configuration management tool that allows you to automate the management of your system configurations. With Ansible, you can define your desired state configuration, and then use playbooks to apply these configurations to your systems. In this section, I will explore how to manage system configurations with Ansible, including how to write playbooks, manage files, install packages, and manage services.

Writing Ansible Playbooks

Ansible playbooks are files that define a set of tasks to be executed on one or more remote systems. Playbooks are written in YAML format and consist of a series of plays, where each play defines a set of tasks to be executed on a set of hosts. Here's an example playbook that installs the Apache Ib server on a set of Ubuntu servers:

YAML

```
---
- name: Install Apache Ib Server
  hosts: Ibservers
  become: true
  tasks:
   - name: Install Apache
     apt:
       name: apache2
       state: present
   - name: Start Apache
     service:
       name: apache2
       state: started
```

In the above example, the playbook defines a set of tasks that install the Apache Ib server on a set of hosts, and then start the Apache service.

Managing Files with Ansible

One of the most common tasks when managing system configurations is managing files. Ansible provides several modules for managing files, including copy, template, and file. Here's an example playbook that copies a file to a set of hosts:

YAML

```
---
- name: Copy Configuration File
  hosts: Ibservers
  become: true
  tasks:
   - name: Copy Config File
     copy:
       src: files/config_file.conf
       dest: /etc/my_app/config_file.conf
```

In the above example, the playbook uses the copy module to copy a file from the local file system to the remote hosts.

Managing Packages with Ansible

Another common task when managing system configurations is managing packages. Ansible provides several modules for managing packages, including apt, yum, and dnf. Here's an example playbook that installs a package on a set of hosts:

YAML

```
---
- name: Install Package
  hosts: Ibservers
  become: true
  tasks:
```

```
  - name: Install Package
    apt:
      name: my_package
      state: present
```

In the above example, the playbook uses the apt module to install a package on the remote hosts.

Managing Services with Ansible

Another common task when managing system configurations is managing services. Ansible provides several modules for managing services, including systemd, service, and win_service. Here's an example playbook that starts a service on a set of hosts:

YAML

```
---
- name: Start Service
  hosts: Ibservers
  become: true
  tasks:
    - name: Start Service
      service:
        name: my_service
        state: started
```

In the above example, the playbook uses the service module to start a service on the remote hosts.

Conclusion

Ansible is a powerful configuration management tool that allows you to automate the management of your system configurations. With Ansible, you can define your desired state configuration, and then use playbooks to apply these configurations to your systems. In this section, I have explored how to manage system configurations with Ansible, including how to write playbooks, manage files, install packages, and manage services. By following these best practices, you can use Ansible to effectively manage your system configurations and ensure that your systems are always in the desired state.

IV.II Automating network device configurations with Ansible

Network devices such as routers and switches are critical components of modern IT infrastructures, and the configuration of these devices is often complex and time-consuming. Ansible, a popular configuration management tool, can help simplify the management of network device configurations by automating the process. In this section, I will explore how to automate network device configurations with Ansible, including how to write playbooks, manage device inventory, and use Ansible modules specific to network devices.

Writing Ansible Playbooks for Network Devices

Ansible playbooks are files that define a set of tasks to be executed on one or more remote systems. Playbooks for network devices are similar to those for servers, but they use modules specific to network devices to manage the configuration of the devices. Here's an example playbook that configures the hostname and domain name on a Cisco router:

YAML

```
---
- name: Configure Router Hostname and Domain Name
  hosts: routers
  gather_facts: no
  become: yes
  tasks:
   - name: Set Hostname
    ios_command:
      commands:
        - hostname {{ inventory_hostname }}
   - name: Set Domain Name
    ios_config:
```

```
  lines:
    - ip domain name mydomain.com
```

In the above example, the playbook defines a set of tasks that configure the hostname and domain name on a set of Cisco routers.

Managing Device Inventory

To use Ansible to manage network device configurations, you need to define an inventory of your network devices. The inventory is a simple text file that lists the network devices you want to manage, along with their IP addresses or hostnames. Here's an example inventory file:

```
[routers]
router1 ansible_host=192.168.1.1
router2 ansible_host=192.168.1.2
```

In the above example, the inventory defines a group of routers and their IP addresses.

Using Ansible Modules for Network Devices

Ansible provides several modules specific to network devices, including modules for managing configuration files, interfaces, VLANs, and more. These modules use the same simple syntax as other Ansible modules but are tailored for managing network devices. Here's an example playbook that configures a VLAN on a Cisco switch:

YAML

```
---
- name: Configure VLAN on Switch
  hosts: switches
  gather_facts: no
  become: yes
  tasks:
    - name: Create VLAN
      ios_vlan:
```

```
    vlan_id: 100
    name: myvlan
```

In the above example, the playbook uses the ios_vlan module to configure a VLAN on a Cisco switch.

Conclusion

Automating network device configurations with Ansible can help simplify the management of complex and time-consuming network configurations. In this section, I explored how to write Ansible playbooks for network devices, manage device inventory, and use Ansible modules specific to network devices. By following these best practices, you can use Ansible to effectively manage your network device configurations and ensure that your network is always in the desired state.

IV.III Managing cloud infrastructure with Ansible

As more and more organizations move their infrastructure to the cloud, the need for effective management and automation of cloud infrastructure grows. Ansible, a popular configuration management tool, can be used to manage a cloud infrastructure in a variety of environments, including Amazon Ib Services (AWS), Microsoft Azure, and Google Cloud Platform (GCP). In this section, I will explore how to use Ansible to manage cloud infrastructure, including how to create playbooks, manage cloud resources, and use Ansible modules specific to cloud platforms.

Writing Ansible Playbooks for Cloud Infrastructure

Ansible playbooks are files that define a set of tasks to be executed on one or more remote systems. Playbooks for cloud infrastructure are similar to those for servers or network devices, but use modules specific to cloud platforms to manage the infrastructure. Here's an example playbook that creates an EC2 instance on AWS:

YAML

```
---
- name: Create EC2 Instance
  hosts: localhost
  gather_facts: no
  become: no
  vars:
    image_id: ami-0c55b159cbfafe1f0
    instance_type: t2.micro
    security_group: mysecuritygroup
    subnet_id: mysubnet
  tasks:
    - name: Create EC2 Instance
```

```
  ec2:
    image: "{{ image_id }}"

instance_type: "{{ instance_type }}"

security_group: "{{ security_group }}"
    subnet_id: "{{ subnet_id }}"

assign_public_ip: yes
    register: ec2_instance
   - name: Print EC2 Instance IP
    debug:
      var: ec2_instance.instances[0].public_ip_address
```

In the above example, the playbook defines a set of tasks that create an EC2 instance on AWS and output its public IP address.

Managing Cloud Resource Inventory

To use Ansible to manage cloud infrastructure, you need to define an inventory of your cloud resources. The inventory can be created using an Ansible inventory file, or dynamically using cloud-specific inventory plugins. Here's an example inventory file for AWS:

```
[aws]
ec2_instance                    ansible_host=ec2-xxx-xxx-xxx-
xxx.compute-1.amazonaws.com
```

In the above example, the inventory defines an EC2 instance in the aws group.

Using Ansible Modules for Cloud Infrastructure

Ansible provides several modules specific to cloud platforms, including modules for managing EC2 instances, S3 buckets, Azure resources, and more. These modules use the same simple syntax as other Ansible modules but are tailored for managing cloud resources. Here's an example playbook that creates an S3 bucket on AWS:

YAML

```
---
- name: Create S3 Bucket
  hosts: localhost
  gather_facts: no
  become: no
  tasks:
   - name: Create S3 Bucket
    s3_bucket:
      name: mybucket
      region: us-east-1
```

In the above example, the playbook uses the s3_bucket module to create an S3 bucket on AWS.

Conclusion

Managing cloud infrastructure with Ansible can help simplify the management of complex and time-consuming cloud resources. In this section, I explored how to write Ansible playbooks for cloud infrastructure, manage cloud resource inventory, and use Ansible modules specific to cloud platforms. By following these best practices, you can use Ansible to effectively manage your cloud infrastructure and ensure that your resources are always in the desired state.

IV.IV Using Ansible Tower for centralized management and control

As organizations grow and their IT infrastructure becomes more complex, managing infrastructure configuration and deployments becomes increasingly challenging. Ansible Tower, an Ib-based interface for Ansible, provides a centralized management and control platform for Ansible playbooks and roles. In this section, I'll explore how Ansible Tower can simplify the management and deployment of Ansible playbooks, enhance collaboration, and provide a scalable solution for organizations of all sizes.

Benefits of Ansible Tower
Ansible Tower provides several key benefits for organizations looking to streamline their IT infrastructure management:

- **Centralized Management and Control:** With Ansible Tower, IT administrators can create and manage their Ansible playbooks from a centralized Ib interface. This allows them to easily manage the configuration and deployment of infrastructure across multiple servers and environments.

- **Role-Based Access Control:** Ansible Tower allows organizations to define access controls to their Ansible playbooks and inventories, ensuring that only authorized personnel have access to sensitive infrastructure.

- **Enhanced Collaboration:** Ansible Tower's Ib interface enables multiple IT administrators to collaborate on the same playbook, role, or inventory. This enhances collaboration and helps ensure consistency across the IT infrastructure.

- **Scalability:** Ansible Tower can be used to manage and deploy Ansible playbooks across multiple environments, enabling organizations to scale their IT infrastructure management as they grow.

Using Ansible Tower

Ansible Tower provides an Ib-based interface for managing Ansible playbooks, roles, and inventories. To get started with Ansible Tower, follow these steps:

- **Install Ansible Tower:** Ansible Tower is available as a commercial product from Ansible. Follow the instructions provided with the installation package to install and configure Ansible Tower.

- **Create an Ansible Project:** An Ansible project is a collection of Ansible playbooks and roles. To create an Ansible project in Ansible Tower, navigate to the Projects section of the Ib interface and click the "Add Project" button. Enter the name and details of the project and provide the location of the project files.

- **Create an Ansible Inventory:** An Ansible inventory is a list of hosts and groups that are managed by Ansible. To create an inventory, navigate to the Inventories section of the Ib interface and click the "Add Inventory" button. Enter the name and details of the inventory and provide the list of hosts and groups.

- **Create an Ansible Job Template:** An Ansible job template is a configuration that defines the playbooks, roles, and inventories to be used in an Ansible job. To create a job template, navigate to the Templates section of the Ib interface and click the "Add Job Template" button. Enter the name and details of the job template and provide the project, inventory, and other settings.

- **Launch an Ansible Job:** To launch an Ansible job using the job template, navigate to the Jobs section of the Ib interface and click the "Launch" button. Select the job template and provide any additional settings required. The job will be launched and its status will be displayed in the Jobs section.

Conclusion

Ansible Tower provides a centralized management and control platform for Ansible playbooks, roles, and inventories. It simplifies the management and deployment of IT infrastructure, enhances collaboration, and provides a scalable solution for organizations of all sizes. By following the steps outlined in this section, you can get started with Ansible Tower and begin using its powerful features to manage and deploy your IT infrastructure.

V. ADVANCED TOPICS IN ANSIBLE

V.I Customizing and extending
Ansible with modules and plugins

Ansible is an open-source automation tool that simplifies configuration management, application deployment, and task automation. It is widely used in IT operations to streamline tasks and improve productivity. Ansible provides a rich set of built-in modules and plugins that can be used to automate tasks on remote hosts. However, sometimes the built-in modules and plugins may not be sufficient to fulfill specific requirements. In such cases, Ansible provides the ability to customize and extend modules and plugins. In this section, I will explore the process of customizing and extending Ansible with modules and plugins.

Ansible Modules
Ansible modules are scripts or programs that are executed on remote hosts to perform specific tasks. They are responsible for communicating with remote hosts, gathering information, and performing actions. Ansible provides a rich set of built-in modules that cover a wide range of tasks, such as managing users, packages, services, and files. However, sometimes the built-in modules may not be sufficient to fulfill specific requirements. In such cases, I can create our custom modules.

Creating Custom Modules
Creating a custom module is straightforward. A module is simply a script or program that follows a specific structure and returns a JSON-formatted output. Here are the steps to create a custom module:

Choose a name for the module and create a file with that name in the library/ directory of your Ansible project.

Write the module code in the file. The code should follow the Ansible module structure, which includes the following:

- **Module documentation**, which describes the module's purpose, parameters, and returns values.
- **Module argument specification**, which defines the module's input parameters and their data types.
- **Module logic**, which performs the module's tasks and generates the output.
- Save the file and make it executable.

Test the module by invoking it with the ansible command and passing the required parameters.

Here is an example of a custom module that creates a user on a remote host:

YAML

```python
# library/create_user.py
#!/usr/bin/env python
from ansible.module_utils.basic import AnsibleModule
def main():
    module = AnsibleModule(

argument_spec=dict(

username=dict(required=True, type='str'),

password=dict(required=True, type='str', no_log=True),
        state=dict(default='present', choices=['present', 'absent']),
    ),

supports_check_mode=True,
    )

    username = module.params['username']
    password = module.params['password']
    state = module.params['state']
```

```python
    if module.check_mode:

module.exit_json(changed=False)

    if state == 'present':
        # Logic to create user
        changed = True
    else:
        # Logic to delete user
        changed = True


module.exit_json(changed=changed)

if __name__ == '__main__':
    main()
```

This module takes three parameters: username, password, and state. It creates or deletes a user on the remote host based on the state parameter.

Using Custom Modules

Once you have created a custom module, you can use it in your Ansible playbooks like any other built-in module. Simply specify the name of the module in the module field of the task definition, and pass any required parameters as key-value pairs in the args field. For example:

YAML

```yaml
# playbook.yml

- name: Create user
  hosts: all
  tasks:
    - name: Create user
      become: yes
      module: create_user
      args:
```

```
username: alice
password: secret
state: present
```

Customizing and extending Ansible with plugins

Ansible plugins are Python modules that extend Ansible's functionality. However, sometimes the built-in modules may not be sufficient to meet specific requirements. In such cases, Ansible provides the ability to customize and extend its functionality with plugins. In this section, I will explore the process of customizing and extending Ansible with plugins.

What are Ansible Plugins?
Ansible plugins are Python modules that extend Ansible's functionality. Plugins can be used to modify the behavior of Ansible at various stages of its execution. Ansible provides four types of plugins: action, connection, inventory, and lookup.

- **Action Plugins**
Action plugins are used to execute actions on remote hosts. They are executed after the playbook has been parsed and before it is executed. Action plugins can be used to modify the behavior of built-in modules or to add new functionality.

- **Connection Plugins**
Connection plugins are used to establish connections to remote hosts. They define the protocol used to communicate with remote hosts and provide the necessary credentials. Connection plugins can be used to support new protocols or to customize the behavior of existing protocols.

- **Inventory Plugins**
Inventory plugins are used to dynamically generate the inventory of hosts that Ansible should manage. Inventory plugins can be used to read inventory from external sources or to generate inventory dynamically based on various criteria.

- **Lookup Plugins**

Lookup plugins are used to retrieve data from various sources. They can be used to retrieve data from external sources or to transform data retrieved from other sources.

Creating Custom Plugins

Creating a custom plugin is straightforward. A plugin is simply a Python module that follows a specific structure and implements specific methods. Here are the steps to create a custom plugin:

1. Choose a name for the plugin and create a Python module with that name in the appropriate directory of your Ansible project. For example, if you are creating an action plugin, create a Python module with the *.py* extension in the *action_plugins/* directory.

2. Write the plugin code in the module. The code should follow the Ansible plugin structure, which includes the following:

- **Plugin documentation**, which describes the plugin's purpose and behavior.
- **Plugin initialization**, which initializes the plugin's state and sets default values for its configuration parameters.
- **Plugin methods**, which implement the plugin's functionality.
- **Save the module**.

Here is an example of a custom action plugin that prints a message before and after a task is executed:

```
# action_plugins/print_message.py

from ansible.plugins.action import ActionBase

class ActionModule(ActionBase):
    def run(self, tmp=None, task_vars=None):
        # Print a message before the task is executed

self._display.banner('Executing task: %s' % self._task.get_name())

        # Execute the task
```

```
result = super(ActionModule, self).run(tmp, task_vars)

# Print a message after the task is executed

self._display.banner('Task          completed:          %s'          %
self._task.get_name())

    return result
```

This plugin extends the behavior of built-in modules by printing a message before and after a task is executed.

Using Custom Plugins

Once you have created a custom plugin, you can use it in your Ansible playbooks by specifying its name in the appropriate field of the task definition. For example, if you have created an action plugin named print_message, you can use it in a task definition like this:

YAML

```
- name: Example task
  hosts: all
  tasks:
    - name: Task with custom plugin
      print_message:
        module_name: ping
        data:
          host: "{{ inventory_hostname }}"
```

V.II Integrating Ansible with other tools and systems

Ansible is a powerful automation tool that can be used to manage a wide range of systems and infrastructure. However, it's not always enough to work on its own, especially when it comes to complex environments. Therefore, integrating it with other tools and systems can greatly increase its capabilities and provide a more comprehensive automation solution.

Here are some examples of how Ansible can be integrated with other tools and systems:

- **Cloud platforms:** Ansible can be used to manage infrastructure on various cloud platforms such as AWS, Azure, and GCP. It provides modules that allow you to automate the provisioning of resources, manage configurations, and deploy applications.

- **Configuration management tools:** Ansible can be integrated with other configuration management tools such as Puppet and Chef. This allows you to use Ansible to manage tasks that are outside the scope of the other tools or to provide a more robust automation solution.

- **Continuous Integration/Continuous Deployment (CI/CD) tools:** Ansible can be integrated with CI/CD tools like Jenkins, CircleCI, and TravisCI. This allows you to automate the deployment of applications and infrastructure as part of the CI/CD pipeline.

- **Monitoring tools:** Ansible can be integrated with monitoring tools such as Nagios and Zabbix. This allows you to automate the configuration and management of monitoring tools as well as the response to alerts.

- **ChatOps tools:** Ansible can be integrated with chat tools such as Slack and Microsoft Teams. This allows you to use chat interfaces to trigger Ansible automation and to receive notifications of automation results.

- **Version control systems:** Ansible can be integrated with version control systems such as Git and SVN. This allows you to manage Ansible playbooks as code and to use version control workflows for collaboration.

- **Containers and container orchestration tools:** Ansible can be used to manage containerized infrastructure and can be integrated with container orchestration tools such as Kubernetes, Docker Swarm, and OpenShift. This allows you to manage container deployment and configuration as part of your infrastructure automation.

In conclusion, integrating Ansible with other tools and systems can greatly increase its capabilities and provide a more comprehensive automation solution. By leveraging the strengths of other tools, you can create a more powerful and flexible automation system that can handle complex environments with ease.

V.III Managing security and compliance with Ansible

As an automation tool, Ansible can be used to streamline security and compliance processes by automating the implementation of security policies and auditing compliance across an IT infrastructure.

Here are some ways Ansible can help manage security and compliance:

- **Automate Security Hardening:** Ansible can be used to automate the implementation of security hardening standards such as CIS Benchmarks or DISA STIGs. These playbooks can be run on-demand or on a scheduled basis to ensure the infrastructure is compliant with the hardening standards.

- **Continuous Compliance Auditing:** Ansible can be used to automate compliance auditing across the infrastructure. Compliance playbooks can be used to check whether systems are configured correctly and policies are being adhered to. Playbooks can be scheduled to run regularly to ensure that compliance is maintained.

- **Patch Management:** Ansible can be used to automate patch management by providing the ability to easily deploy security patches across the infrastructure. Playbooks can be used to detect vulnerabilities and deploy patches to the affected systems.

- **Configuration Management:** Ansible can be used to manage configuration changes across the infrastructure. Configuration playbooks can be used to ensure that all systems are configured consistently and securely. Changes can be tracked and audited, ensuring that the infrastructure remains secure and compliant.

- **Security Incident Response:** Ansible can be used to automate security incident response procedures. Playbooks can be developed to automate the response to specific types of security incidents, such as detecting and blocking a DDoS attack or locking down a compromised system.

- **Multi-factor Authentication Management:** Ansible can be used to manage multi-factor authentication (MFA) across an infrastructure. MFA playbooks can be used to automate the deployment and configuration of MFA tools such as Duo or Google Authenticator.

- **Security Information and Event Management:** Ansible can be used to integrate with security information and event management (SIEM) tools. Playbooks can be used to automate the transfer of log data to a SIEM tool, as well as to automate the response to security events detected by the SIEM.

In conclusion, Ansible can be used to manage security and compliance across an IT infrastructure by automating the implementation of security policies, continuous compliance auditing, patch management, configuration management, incident response, multi-factor authentication management, and SIEM integration. By using Ansible to automate these processes, organizations can improve their security posture and ensure compliance with regulations and standards.

V.IV Using Ansible for application deployment and orchestration

Ansible is a powerful automation tool that can be used to automate the deployment and orchestration of applications across an infrastructure. In this section, I'll explore some of the benefits of using Ansible for application deployment and orchestration, as well as some best practices for using Ansible to manage your applications.

Benefits of using Ansible for application deployment and orchestration:

- **Consistent Application Deployment:** Ansible can be used to automate the deployment of applications across an infrastructure, ensuring that all deployments are consistent and follow best practices.

- **Improved Application Availability:** Ansible can be used to monitor application health and take action if an application becomes unavailable. Playbooks can be developed to detect issues and automatically restart failed applications.

- **Streamlined Application Management:** Ansible can be used to manage multiple applications across an infrastructure, allowing for centralized management of all applications.

- **Better Resource Utilization:** Ansible can be used to orchestrate application deployments across multiple servers, improving resource utilization and ensuring that applications are deployed to the most appropriate servers.

- **Increased Agility:** Ansible allows for the rapid

deployment of new applications and updates, providing organizations with the agility they need to quickly respond to changing business needs.

Best practices for using Ansible for application deployment and orchestration:

- **Use Roles:** Ansible roles are a powerful way to organize your playbooks and create reusable code. By using roles, you can ensure that your application deployments follow a consistent structure and configuration.

- **Use Templates:** Ansible templates can be used to create dynamic configuration files that are customized for each application deployment. This allows for greater flexibility in application configuration and reduces the need for manual intervention.

- **Use Variables:** Ansible variables can be used to store application configuration data, making it easier to manage and deploy applications across an infrastructure. By using variables, you can ensure that your application deployments are consistent and follow best practices.

- **Use Inventory:** Ansible inventory can be used to manage the servers and other infrastructure components that your applications are deployed on. By using inventory, you can ensure that your applications are deployed to the correct servers and that resources are being utilized efficiently.

- **Use Ansible Tower:** Ansible Tower is a powerful management tool that can be used to manage and orchestrate application deployments across multiple servers. By using Tower, you can automate complex workflows and ensure that your applications are deployed and managed with a high degree of reliability and consistency.

In conclusion, Ansible is a powerful automation tool that can be used to automate the deployment and orchestration of applications across an infrastructure. By using Ansible to manage your applications, you can ensure that your deployments are consistent and follow best practices, improve resource utilization, increase agility, and streamline application management. By following best practices such as using roles, templates, variables, inventory, and Ansible Tower, you can ensure that your application deployments are reliable, consistent, and efficient.

VI. BEST PRACTICES AND TROUBLESHOOTING

VI.I Ansible best practices for code organization and performance

Ansible is a powerful automation tool that can be used to manage and deploy applications across an infrastructure. However, as your Ansible playbooks and roles grow in size and complexity, it becomes increasingly important to follow best practices for code organization and performance to ensure that your code is maintainable, scalable, and efficient.

Here are some best practices for organizing and optimizing your Ansible code:

Organize your code into roles: Roles are a powerful way to organize your Ansible code into reusable components. By creating roles for different tasks and functions, you can simplify your playbook code and reduce duplication.

- **Use variables:** Variables are a key component of any Ansible playbook or role. By using variables, you can customize your code for different environments and deployments. Use variable files to store environment-specific configuration data, and use Ansible Vault to encrypt sensitive data.

- **Use task lists:** Task lists are an easy way to organize your Ansible playbook code into logical steps. By using task lists, you can break your playbook code into smaller, more manageable chunks, making it easier to read and maintain.

- **Use tags:** Tags are a powerful way to organize your Ansible playbook code and improve performance. By using tags, you can selectively run parts of your playbook code, reducing the amount of time it takes to run your playbook.

- **Use handlers:** Handlers are a powerful way to manage changes to your infrastructure. By using handlers, you can trigger specific actions when changes occur, reducing the amount of code you need to write and improving performance.

- **Use conditionals:** Conditionals are a powerful way to customize your Ansible playbook code for different environments and deployments. By using conditionals, you can execute code based on specific criteria, reducing the amount of duplicate code you need to write.

- **Optimize performance:** Ansible can be optimized for performance by reducing the amount of unnecessary code and reducing the number of tasks that need to be executed. Use tags and conditionals to selectively run parts of your code, and use caching to improve performance.

In conclusion, following best practices for code organization and performance is essential for creating maintainable, scalable, and efficient Ansible playbooks and roles. By organizing your code into roles, using variables, task lists, tags, handlers, and conditionals, and optimizing performance, you can ensure that your Ansible code is optimized for performance and maintainability. With these best practices in mind, you can create Ansible code that is flexible, efficient, and easy to maintain.

VI.II Troubleshooting Ansible errors and issues

As with any software, issues, and errors can arise while using Ansible. In this section, I will cover some common Ansible errors and issues and how to troubleshoot them.

How to troubleshoot Ansible errors and issues?

- **Check for syntax errors:** Syntax errors are the most common type of Ansible error. Check your playbook code for any missing brackets or commas, or any other syntax errors. Ansible provides a built-in syntax checker that you can use to check your code for syntax errors.

- **Check your inventory:** Ansible uses an inventory file to specify the hosts and groups that it will manage. Make sure that your inventory file is properly formatted and that all the hosts and groups are defined correctly.

- **Check for SSH connectivity issues:** Ansible uses SSH to connect to remote hosts. Make sure that SSH is properly configured on the remote hosts and that Ansible can connect to the hosts using SSH. Use the "ssh" command to test SSH connectivity.

- **Check for permission issues:** Ansible requires certain permissions to execute tasks on remote hosts. Make sure that the Ansible user has the necessary permissions to execute tasks on the remote hosts.

- **Use verbose mode:** Ansible provides a verbose mode that can be used to display more detailed information about what is happening during playbook execution. Use the "-vvv" option to enable verbose mode.

- **Use the "debug" module:** The "debug" module can be used to display variables and other information during playbook execution. Use the "debug" module to troubleshoot issues and errors in your playbook code.

- **Use the Ansible Tower logs:** If you are using Ansible Tower, you can use the Ansible Tower logs to troubleshoot issues and errors. The Ansible Tower logs provide detailed information about what is happening during playbook execution.

- **Use the Ansible community:** The Ansible community is a great resource for troubleshooting Ansible issues and errors. Use the Ansible mailing list or forums to ask for help from other Ansible users and experts.

In conclusion, troubleshooting Ansible errors and issues can be a complex process, but by following these tips and best practices, you can quickly identify and resolve issues in your Ansible code. Check for syntax errors, inventory issues, SSH connectivity issues, and permission issues, use verbose mode and debug module, and use Ansible Tower logs and the Ansible community for help. With these tools and resources, you can quickly troubleshoot and resolve Ansible issues and errors, and create efficient and reliable Ansible playbooks and roles.

VI.III Scaling Ansible for larger environments

As the size of the infrastructure grows, it can become challenging to manage Ansible at scale. In this section, I will cover some best practices for scaling Ansible for larger environments.

How to scale Ansible for larger environments?

- **Use Ansible Tower:** Ansible Tower is a powerful tool that provides a centralized platform for managing Ansible playbooks and roles. Ansible Tower provides features like job scheduling, role-based access control, and workflow automation, which make it easier to manage Ansible at scale.

- **Use dynamic inventories:** Dynamic inventories allow you to define your inventory in an external data source, like a database or API, rather than a static file. This makes it easier to manage large and dynamic infrastructures.

- **Use Ansible roles:** Ansible roles are a powerful tool for organizing your playbooks and making them more modular. Roles allow you to separate different parts of your playbook into distinct, reusable units, which makes it easier to manage and scale your Ansible codebase.

- **Use parallelism:** Ansible supports the parallel execution of tasks, which can significantly improve performance when managing large infrastructures. Use the "forks" option to control the number of parallel processes that Ansible can use.

- **Use caching:** Ansible can cache facts and task results, which can significantly improve performance when running playbooks repeatedly. Use the "cache" option to enable caching.

- **Use delegation:** Delegation allows you to delegate tasks to a different host or group of hosts. This is useful when you need to perform tasks that require specialized software or hardware.

- **Use Ansible Galaxy:** Ansible Galaxy is a repository of community-contributed roles and playbooks. Use Ansible Galaxy to find pre-built roles and playbooks that you can use to manage your infrastructure.

- **Use Ansible in a containerized environment:** Containerization can make it easier to manage and scale your infrastructure. Use Ansible to manage containers and container orchestration tools like Kubernetes and Docker Swarm.

In conclusion, scaling Ansible for larger environments can be challenging, but by following these best practices, you can create efficient and reliable Ansible playbooks and roles that can manage your infrastructure at scale. Use Ansible Tower, dynamic inventories, Ansible roles, parallelism, caching, delegation, Ansible Galaxy, and containerization to manage and scale your Ansible codebase. With these tools and best practices, you can manage and automate your infrastructure with Ansible, regardless of its size or complexity.

VI.IV Monitoring and reporting with Ansible

With Ansible, you can automate monitoring tasks, generate reports, and trigger alerts when specific conditions are met. In this section, I will cover some best practices for monitoring and reporting with Ansible.

Best practices for monitoring and reporting with Ansible:

- **Use Ansible modules:** Ansible provides a wide range of modules that can be used to automate monitoring tasks. For example, you can use the "shell" module to execute shell commands on remote hosts, the "ping" module to check if a host is alive, or the "nagios" module to interact with Nagios monitoring software.

- **Use Ansible roles:** Ansible roles can be used to organize your monitoring tasks and make them more modular. You can create roles that define specific monitoring tasks, such as checking the status of a service or monitoring disk usage. Roles allow you to reuse code and make it easier to manage and scale your monitoring tasks.

- **Use Ansible Playbooks:** Ansible Playbooks allow you to define a set of tasks that should be executed on a group of hosts. You can use Playbooks to automate your monitoring tasks and generate reports. For example, you can create a playbook that checks the status of all services running on a set of hosts and generates a report that lists the status of each service.

- **Use Ansible Vault:** Ansible Vault is a feature that allows you to encrypt sensitive data, such as login credentials,

API keys, or monitoring configurations. You can use Ansible Vault to store your monitoring configurations securely and avoid exposing sensitive information in your Ansible codebase.

- **Use Ansible Tower:** Ansible Tower provides a centralized platform for managing Ansible Playbooks and Roles. Ansible Tower includes features such as job scheduling, role-based access control, and workflow automation, which make it easier to manage and scale your monitoring tasks.

- **Use monitoring plugins:** Monitoring plugins are pre-built scripts that can be used to check the status of specific services or applications. Ansible supports various monitoring plugins, such as Nagios, Icinga, or Prometheus. You can use monitoring plugins to automate your monitoring tasks and generate reports that provide insights into the health of your infrastructure.

In conclusion, monitoring and reporting with Ansible can be powerful and efficient when used correctly. By following these best practices, you can automate monitoring tasks, generate reports, and trigger alerts when specific conditions are met. Use Ansible modules, roles, playbooks, Vault, Tower, and monitoring plugins to create efficient and reliable monitoring workflows with Ansible. With these tools and best practices, you can monitor your infrastructure proactively and avoid costly downtime.

VII. CONCLUSION

VII.I Summary of key concepts and skills

Ansible is a popular open-source automation tool that is widely used to automate IT infrastructure tasks such as configuration management, application deployment, and orchestration. It uses simple and declarative language to define tasks, which makes it easy to learn and use. In this section, I will summarize the key concepts and skills needed to effectively use Ansible.

A summary of the key concepts and skills needed to use Ansible effectively:

- **Inventory:** An inventory is a list of hosts that Ansible manages. It can be a simple text file or a dynamic inventory that pulls information from cloud providers, virtualization platforms, or configuration management databases. The inventory is the foundation of Ansible's automation and orchestration capabilities.

- **Playbooks:** Playbooks are Ansible's configuration files that define the tasks to be executed on a set of hosts. Playbooks are written in YAML and can include tasks, variables, conditions, loops, and handlers. Playbooks are the main building blocks of Ansible automation and are used to define complex workflows.

- **Modules:** Modules are Ansible's building blocks that carry out the tasks defined in Playbooks. Modules are used to perform actions such as installing packages, copying files, or managing users and groups. Ansible provides hundreds of built-in modules, and users can also write custom modules.

- **Tasks:** Tasks are the individual actions that Ansible

performs on a host. A task can be a module, a command, or a script that Ansible executes on a host. Tasks are defined in Playbooks and are executed in the order they are defined.

- **Variables:** Variables are used to store data that can be used across different parts of a Playbook. Variables can be defined at the playbook, role, or task level. Variables can be used to set values for module parameters, define conditions, or store configuration data.

- **Templates:** Templates are files that are used to generate dynamic configuration files on the managed hosts. Templates use Jinja2, a templating language that allows you to generate configuration files based on the values of variables defined in the playbook.

- **Roles:** Roles are a way of organizing Playbooks and tasks into reusable units. Roles can be used to define the tasks and configuration needed for a specific application or service. Roles can also include templates, files, and variables.

- **Handlers:** Handlers are tasks that are triggered by a notification sent by another task. Handlers are defined in Playbooks and are executed only when the corresponding task generates a notification. Handlers are often used to restart services or reload configuration files.

- **Tags:** Tags are used to selectively execute tasks in a Playbook. Tags are defined at the task level and can be used to run specific tasks based on the tags assigned to them.

- **Conditionals:** Conditionals are used to define conditions that determine whether a task should be executed or skipped. Conditionals can be defined using Jinja2 syntax and can use variables, comparisons, and logical operators.

In conclusion, Ansible is a powerful automation tool that simplifies the management of IT infrastructure. To use Ansible effectively, you need to understand the key concepts and skills such as inventory, playbooks, modules, tasks, variables, templates, roles, handlers, tags, and conditionals. By mastering these concepts and skills, you can create efficient and reliable automation workflows that save time and reduce errors.

VII.II Final thoughts on mastering Ansible

Mastering Ansible requires more than just understanding the syntax and features of the tool. Here are some final thoughts on mastering Ansible:

- **Start with the basics:** If you're new to Ansible, start with the basics. Learn the key concepts such as inventory, playbooks, modules, tasks, variables, templates, roles, handlers, tags, and conditionals. Practice writing simple Playbooks and gradually build up to more complex workflows.

- **Learn by doing:** Ansible is best learned by doing. Create your automation workflows and experiment with different configurations. The more you use Ansible, the more you'll understand how it works and how to optimize your workflows.

- **Use best practices:** Use Ansible best practices to organize your code, manage variables, and optimize performance. Adopt standard naming conventions, use roles to organize your Playbooks, and use version control to manage your code.

- **Test your Playbooks:** Test your Playbooks in a development or test environment before running them in production. Use Ansible's dry-run mode to test your Playbooks without actually executing them. Use Ansible's built-in testing tools such as Ansible-lint and Molecule to validate your Playbooks.

- **Keep it simple:** Ansible is designed to simplify IT automation. Keep your Playbooks simple and easy to understand. Use descriptive variable names, avoid complex conditionals, and break up long Playbooks into smaller, reusable roles.

- **Stay up to date:** Ansible is constantly evolving, with new features and improvements being added all the time. Stay up to date with the latest releases, read the Ansible documentation, and participate in the Ansible community.

In conclusion, mastering Ansible requires more than just understanding the syntax and features of the tool. It requires practice, experimentation, and a commitment to using best practices. By following these tips, you can become an Ansible expert and create efficient and reliable automation workflows that save time and reduce errors.

EPILOGUE

Congratulations! You've made it to the end of "Mastering Ansible: A Comprehensive Guide to Automating Configuration Management and Deployment". I hope that this book has helped you become a master of Ansible and empowered you to automate your infrastructure as code.

I've covered a lot of ground in this book, from the basics of Ansible to advanced topics such as modules, plugins, roles, and dynamic inventory. I've shown you how to write efficient, modular, and reusable playbooks, and how to use Ansible to automate a wide range of tasks, from provisioning servers to deploying applications. I've also provided best practices, tips, and tricks to help you work more effectively and efficiently with Ansible.

But our journey with Ansible doesn't end here. Ansible is a dynamic and evolving tool, with new features and capabilities being added all the time. I encourage you to stay up-to-date with the latest developments in Ansible, to contribute to the Ansible community, and to share your knowledge and experience with others.

I also hope that this book has inspired you to think differently about infrastructure management and automation. Ansible is not just a tool, it's a philosophy that emphasizes simplicity, transparency, and collaboration. It's a way of thinking about infrastructure as code, and about automation as a means of empowering humans to be more creative and innovative. I believe that Ansible can help you achieve this vision, and I look forward to seeing what you'll do with it.

Thank you for reading "***Mastering Ansible:*** *A Comprehensive Guide to Automating Configuration Management and Deployment*". I hope that you've found it useful and informative, and I wish you all the best in your automation journey.

ABOUT THE AUTHOR

Ghada Atef

Ghada Atef is not just a Linux expert; she's a seasoned author and dedicated online instructor with a passion for sharing knowledge. With over twelve years of industry experience, Ghada has become a trusted authority in Linux administration, IT automation, and Scripting.

As an accomplished author, Ghada has penned six insightful books, spanning topics from Linux administration to cutting-edge IT automation. Her commitment to education extends to her role as an online instructor, where she's crafted two enriching courses, guiding students worldwide on their learning journeys.

Ghada's work is guided by principles of integrity, excellence, innovation, collaboration, and impact. Her unwavering commitment to delivering the highest quality, professionalism, and value to her clients, readers, and students is truly remarkable.

Beyond her impressive credentials, Ghada is driven by a larger mission—to utilize her skills and expertise to create a positive impact on a global scale. Her dedication to continuous growth and learning is evident in her work, and she remains excited about the journey ahead.

BOOKS BY THIS AUTHOR

Unofficial Red Hat Certified System Administrator Rhcsa 8 & 9 (Ex200) Exam Preparation: Six Complete Rhcsa 8 & 9 Practice Exams With Answers

Are you looking to become a Red Hat Certified System Administrator (RHCSA)? Do you want to test your knowledge and skills before taking the exam? Look no further than "Unofficial Red Hat Certified System Administrator RHCSA 8 & 9 (EX200) Exam Preparation: Six Complete RHCSA 8 & 9 Practice Exams with Answers"!

This book is your ultimate guide to preparing for the RHCSA exam. With six complete practice exams, you'll have the opportunity to test your knowledge and hone your skills in a real-world environment. Each exam covers all the topics and objectives of the RHCSA exam for RHEL 8 and 9, so you can be confident that you're fully prepared for the real thing.

Unofficial Red Hat Rhcsa (Ex200) Exam Preparation 2023: Six Complete Rhcsa (Ex200) Practice Exams With Answers (Third Edition)

Looking to ace the Red Hat RHCSA 9 (EX200) exam? Look no further than the "Unofficial Red Hat RHCSA (EX200) Exam Preparation 2023" book. With six complete practice exams for RHCSA 9, this book is the ultimate study resource for anyone preparing to take the RHCSA exam. Whether you're a beginner or an experienced professional, these practice exams will test your knowledge and skills, giving you the confidence you need to pass the RHCSA exam with flying colors. With answers and detailed explanations included, you'll be able to review and strengthen your understanding of key concepts, commands, and techniques. Don't take the RHCSA exam without this essential study guide!

Unofficial Rhcsa 8 & 9 (Ex200) Complete Reference: Rhel 8 & 9

This book is a reference for anyone seeking to learn Linux administration or pass the RHCSA (EX200) exam. This book is a rapid-track course for Red Hat System Administration Certificate and a good reference for the RHCSA exam (EX200) study points.

Mastering Ubuntu: A Comprehensive Guide To Linux's Favorite Distribution

This comprehensive guide is the perfect resource for anyone looking to gain a deep understanding of Ubuntu, from beginners to experienced users. With clear and concise explanations, practical examples, and hands-on exercises, this book will guide you through every aspect of Ubuntu, from installation and configuration to advanced system administration, network setup, and security.

"Mastering Ubuntu" covers all the essential topics, including package management, software installation, network setup, and security, providing you with the knowledge and skills to become a proficient Ubuntu user. You'll learn how to customize your desktop, manage users and groups, automate tasks, and secure your system from unauthorized access.

Learn Pycharm Ide For Kids: Using Pycharm

Python Ide Community Edition

Looking for a fun and engaging way to learn Python programming? Look no further than "Learn PyCharm IDE for Kids: Using PyCharm Python IDE Community Edition"! This comprehensive guide is specifically designed to teach young programmers how to use PyCharm, a popular Python Integrated Development Environment (IDE), to create amazing projects.

With step-by-step instructions, colorful illustrations, and real-world examples, kids will learn how to write and execute Python code, work with variables and data types, use conditional statements and loops, and much more.

By the end of this book, young programmers will have the skills and knowledge they need to take their coding to the next level and create their own amazing projects. So why wait? Start your coding journey today with "Learn PyCharm IDE for Kids: Using PyCharm Python IDE Community Edition"!

Learn Python Essentials: For Newbie Python Developers & Data Scientists

Through this book, I will teach you the basics of Python step by step by simplifying complex concepts into their simplest forms.

Mastering Ansible: A Comprehensive Guide To Automating Configuration Management And Deployment

"Mastering Ansible: A Comprehensive Guide to Automating Configuration Management and Deployment" is an in-depth guide to Ansible, a popular open-source tool for automating infrastructure as code.

The book covers everything from the basics of Ansible to advanced topics such as modules, plugins, roles, and dynamic inventory. It provides detailed guidance on how to write efficient, modular, and reusable playbooks, and how to use Ansible to automate a wide range of tasks, from provisioning servers to deploying applications.

The book also includes best practices, tips, and tricks for working effectively with Ansible, as well as use cases and real-world examples.

Whether you're a beginner or an experienced user, "Mastering Ansible" will help you become a master of Ansible and take your automation skills to the next level.

THANK YOU!

As we come to the end of this journey, I want to express my heartfelt gratitude to everyone who made this book possible.

To my family, for their unwavering support and encouragement throughout this endeavor. Your belief in me has been my greatest motivation.

To my friends and colleagues, for your insights, feedback, and discussions that helped shape this guide into what it is today.

To the open-source community and the dedicated educators at Red Hat, whose passion for Linux and technology continues to inspire me.

To you, the reader, for choosing this book as your companion on the path to learn Ansible.

www.ingramcontent.com/pod-product-compliance
Lightning Source LLC
LaVergne TN
LVHW051248050326
832903LV00028B/2648

* 9 7 9 8 3 8 6 4 8 1 8 7 2 *